Randy Ran

A Leadership Paradox: Influencing Others by Defining Yourself

Revised Edition

by

Greg Robinson
with Mark Rose

authorHOUSE™

1663 LIBERTY DRIVE, SUITE 200
BLOOMINGTON, INDIANA 47403
(800) 839-8640
WWW.AUTHORHOUSE.COM

First published by AuthorHouse 01/09/06

ISBN: 1-4208-1422-2 (e)
ISBN: 1-4184-8515-2 (sc)

Library of Congress Control Number: 2004095687

Printed in the United States of America
Bloomington, Indiana

This book is printed on acid-free paper.

Table of Contents

Introduction

Each day, the sun rises on a world that grows less distant. Every moment, technology compresses time and space to create a closeness never before experienced by the people of the world. With this closeness comes a dramatic increase in the complexity of life. This complexity grows out of the interaction of people who are different. And this difference creates uncertainty because the closeness occurs in a time in which freedom and democracy hold court. There is no king to rule over the masses. Most have the choice to cooperate or to compete. Thus, the only hope of a sustainable future lies in our attempts to live with integrity and trust in one another.

These words could be the beginning of any story. But this book is a different kind of story: a story about the search for effective leadership. This book is the story of one person's search for wisdom and truth, yet it holds something of every person's story. For the truth is, we are all more alike than we are different.

A fundamental assumption in most of the literature on leadership is that a few will need to control the many. Looking backward over history, a subtle belief has remained through revolutions, reformations and revivals--the belief that someone must tell the masses how to live, arising from a fundamental mistrust of others and of self. This assumption leads to a search for power but with an either/or mindset: *if I have power, then others cannot have as much as me or they will be a threat.* Such leadership results in anxious organizations with limited ability to learn and change. However, there is an alternative, paradoxical way to understand leadership. This alternative way of leadership called "leadership by self-differentiation" has its roots in Dr. Edwin Friedman's family systems theory. This goes beyond just self-knowledge. Self-differentiated or self-defined leaders are those who can set their own direction, regulate their own anxiety and can stay connected while not responding to the anxious demands of others. It is critical for these leaders to learn to face their fears, challenge their assumptions and thus be able to change their self-perception. *A Leadership Paradox* outlines such an alternative view of leadership and provides a model for achieving differentiated (defined) leadership.

Purpose of This Book

For those readers who are leaders already, this book will call to mind the nobility of your position. Those around you are desperate for a depth of character that reminds them that there is more than what can be perceived by the senses. Something of value exists within each of us. A leader can see this in times of great chaos and will not allow others to deny the value they possess. To remind individuals of that personal value is to provide a great service, as everyone needs that recognition at some time in his or her life.

To be such a leader, you must let go of the need for certainty and control. Reaching a place beyond the siren call of control and certainty will require a battle of enormous proportions. For such a place is accessible only through the discovery of your own value, hidden just beyond the shadows of your fears. Thus, the foundational premise of this book is a paradox: Leadership is primarily an effort to understand and change yourself. Defining yourself, rather than attempting to change others, is what offers the greatest point of leverage in an organization.

For readers that have ambitions toward leadership, the path will be the same. These pages suggest the kinds of questions leaders must ask. This book will share our own difficult experiences with impatience and with seeking power and position. Even more, this book will reveal the authors' enthusiasm for leadership as a way of being—not as a taskmaster mercilessly driving a person into actions they neither respect nor value. For leadership gained by cunning or domination will lead only to emptiness. Leadership cannot be hurried. It can be gained only in the patience of listening, both to yourself and to others.

More on the Purpose of This Book

This book will be successful if those who read it begin to ask different kinds of questions. We live in a time that requires leaders to ask important questions that reveal the depth and substance of the issues that organizations face. Although these are not the primary questions of this book, Dee Hock, founder of Visa International, asks two questions that frame the impetus of this book:

1. Why are organizations increasingly unable to manage their affairs?
2. Why are individuals increasingly in conflict with and alienated from the organizations of which they are apart?[1]

These are questions of substance. The truth is that the institutions of society are increasingly proving more damaging, not more helpful, to those who exist within them. The lack of authenticity and congruency created by systems of command and control breed fear in organizations. All of us—whether king or servant, leader or follower—are being made something less by our participation in systems that are based on fear, rather than freedom. Moreover, these systems will continue unabated if leaders, formal and informal, do not ask different questions and intentionally take different actions. History has proven that the masses will revolt when power is in the hands of a chosen few who create a system that works only for them. The problem is that with each revolt, the symptoms are relieved but the root issues are rarely addressed. This book provides an approach to effective leadership in organizations that aspire to long-term health rather than the use of bandages and aspirin.

Book Overview

Chapter 1 begins with a definition of leadership and the three roles of effective leaders in organizations. These are not the only roles effective leaders play, but some not usually considered. Chapter 2 more clearly defines the central question of this book: In this age of rapid change, does all change actually produce progress? Leadership is a primary element in answering this question. The quality of leadership in organizations will determine the extent to which change is reactive versus intentional and sustainable. This chapter also extends a new perspective on leadership that was first proposed by Dr. Edwin Friedman. Chapter 3 describes the central dynamic in the differentiation (defining) process. The emerging roles that leaders are being called to play require a particular mindset, character and attitude. The learning model of differentiation (defining) describes the on-going process involved in the profound change leaders must be willing to pursue. In Chapter 4, one of the authors describes what he has learned about the differentiation (defining) process through his own life's experiences, as he has sought greater awareness and intentionality in both work and religious life. Chapter 5 outlines the four core learning abilities that allow you to recognize and participate in the learning process, which is an enabler of self-definition. In Chapter 6, the focus changes from defining yourself to helping others define themselves. There are at least four opportunities for leaders to help others in this self-defining process: Awareness, Clarity, Courageous Connection, and Curiosity.

The next two chapters use two case studies to illustrate how organizations can begin to build the conditions to promote differentiated (defined) learning in organizational life. Both cases come from work within a Fortune 500 energy company. Chapter 7 describes the story of developing a mindset for leadership and continuous learning in an internal Information Technology Consulting

Company. In Appendix B, the leader of this organization, Brent Coussens, offers his perspective on facilitating the conditions that allow people to grow into mature individuals. In Chapter 8, the second case study examines how this company's Safety and Loss Control groups have pursued a learning-based change initiative by focusing on how to increase functional managers' capacity to learn. The central learning model presented in this book was the guiding model of this change effort. The learning model provided a framework for the managers to reframe how they interacted with each other. Appendix C highlights an interview with the leader of this effort, Paul Hunter. Finally, the conclusion of this book suggests the next steps needed to develop a model of differentiated (defined) leadership. In Appendix A, we provide an assessment with some questions to help you evaluate the quality of your interactions with others. The goal of this assessment is to give you a starting point and then to watch for improvement as you become more intentional with your actions.

The Pursuit of Freedom

Why are these questions about the quality of your interactions important? For any organization to have a sustainable future, it must be based on freedom, rather than mistrust. For too long, humans have organized themselves around mistrust and the fear that results. In most organizations, information is hoarded, behavior is regulated through rigid rules, and managers are socialized into thinking their job is to protect the company from the abuses of the workers.

We find ourselves in an age that will not settle for more of the same. This dissatisfaction is more than a passing whim. It is the consequence of a flawed system of thought that no longer remains hidden. New technology has connected people of the world, and in doing so, it has revealed the deep problems in most forms of contemporary organizations. A novel approach would be to organize around maturity and trust. Freedom to participate fully in the system is necessary for sustainability.

For most of Western history there has been a ravenous search for freedom—from hunger, from an oppressive government, from ignorance, or from a god that could not be entirely understood. The basic flaw of these kinds of "freedoms" is that they are grounded in fear of anticipated consequences. And the search for this kind of freedom has reached its pinnacle in the modern age. This type of search must be abandoned. There is no sustainable freedom from something. Rather, we must learn to see the system processes all around us and find the courage to act with freedom in them. Acting on our freedom is an act of courage. It should never be thought that fear will be completely removed. Taking self-determined action is often accompanied by anxiety. However, the fear this book seeks to illumine and respond to is the debilitating fear that grows from mistrust.

How is this book different from other leadership books?

First, many good books on leadership have identified what characteristics effective leaders possess. Not as many have described how those characteristics are developed. This book provides a learning model for how leaders develop these characteristics. Second, this book calls on leaders to quit trying to manage the consequences of a failed bureaucratic model of organization. It clearly defines the root issues behind the fear, mistrust and immaturity that are holding organizations captive today. Finally, this book is different because it shifts the discussion of leadership away from techniques for changing and commanding others and towards the source of real power – defining oneself.

Overall, this book draws from theology, organizational development, psychology, and educational theory to examine the leader's role in the process of sustainable change. This book focuses on what could be called meta-skills. Rather than prescribe particular answers to issues, meta-skills equip people to discover solutions regardless of the particulars of the situation. Much like reading is an underlying skill for all education, self-differentiation (self-definition) is an underlying learning process that promotes maturity, health, and wisdom. Based on research within a Fortune 500 company over a period of two years, the learning model has been demonstrated as transferable and highly successful in helping leaders intentionally pursue self-differentiation (self-definition).

Intended Audiences:
- Leaders who want more than momentary success.
- Leaders who want to impact their organizations for a greater good.
- Leaders who want to facilitate sustainable change.
- Consultants and coaches who want to do more than find "solutions" to managing the symptoms of ineffective organizations and leadership.
- Teachers of leaders who are interested in nudging their students towards a life time journey of immense value.

Central Theme

Using leadership as a lens, this book promotes sustainable change in three ways. First, it calls for leaders to stop and reflect on how leadership affects change. Second, it provides a model and language for leaders to overcome fear and develop new ways of thinking. Finally, it provides some concrete applications for how the self-defining process works and how it is used in the day to day world of work.

The central message underlying all that follows is that if the changes organizations seek to make are to result in progress to a more sustainable and healthy condition, then leaders must consider the very nature of the changes being made. This agenda requires leaders to start by defining themselves and making profound changes to their understanding of power, privilege and their role as leader.

Definition of Leadership

Leadership is not a new concept. Consequently, the definition that follows should not be interpreted as discounting those theories of leadership already established. Rather, the following chapter highlights ideas that have been less frequently considered. This relationship of leadership and facilitation will provide a lexicon for the discussion that follows.

Chapter 1 - The Role of a Leader

*"Leadership can be thought of as a capacity to define oneself to others in
a way that clarifies and expands a vision of the future."*
Edwin H. Friedman

Like others, this book agrees that leadership is not a position to seek
but a role to fulfill. When viewed through the lens of power, position, and
privilege, leadership is a scarce resource that should be protected. However,
when viewed through a different lens, leadership is a responsibility - a
necessary role that must emerge from each individual regardless of his or
her education, experience, or position in the organization. For sustainable
change to take root, this personal responsibility of leadership needs to exist at
every level in an organization. In order to support this personal responsibility
throughout the organization, leaders will have to play three roles that can be
defined as that of prophet, priest, and, a contemporary title - facilitator. The
two religious images might cause some distress but if you can momentarily
suspend judgment, there is some usefulness in the comparisons.

A *prophet* is a proclaimer. In the Jewish and Christian scriptures, prophets
did at least two things: They spoke with unwavering honesty about the
current condition while also forming a vision of what could be. Even though
their honesty seemed harsh and was always confrontational, the purpose of
their messages was to stimulate people to a new and better way. The prophet
realizes that no journey toward a sustainable future can begin until those who
are to make the journey acknowledge just where they are beginning from.
Honesty is a crucial first step.

This is a critical role of a leader. The foundation of trust so essential to
effective organizations is eroded by the current spin of the so-called official

word. The anxiety of the organization can be amplified by avoiding the simple, unadorned truth. Leaders may fear that their people will turn on them as a result of such honesty. Yet in most cases, allowing members to see the 'what' and the 'why' behind an effort to change calls out the best in people.

The prophet's role is not just to confront others with the truth. It also involves trying to build a vision of what could be. A critical component of the prophet's message is that individual choices help elicit the vision. This view of leadership is a long way from the paternalistic view, in which the leader wants to tell others what to do. In comparison, leaders that create the awareness of choices empower their organizations to be mature and thus more sustainable.

The term *priest* is another borrowed religious image and the second role a leader has to play. The greatest gift of the priest is his or her concern with reminding people of who they are. Too many things in life distract individuals from who they really are. We live in an age in which people allow the fragmentation of their society and their own experiences to define who they are.

> *Ultimately, the facilitator seeks to leave those persons he or she helps better equipped to continue on unassisted.*

Leaders are at their best when they see the value in the people around them and call on those people to remember that value. It is easy to forget your own value. Individuals in organizations experience much "dis-ease" when there are no leaders who realize this role. People who do not know their individual value—and their value to the organization—will be swept away trying to prove it. Individuals will forget that value is experienced when they are helpful. When individuals forget their value, they will try to prove their worth by looking better than someone else. As a result, information will be hoarded and opportunities for improvement will fail to materialize. Silos will grow and territories will be drawn. Soon, the organization will be hamstrung by its own fragmentation. All of this can be avoided if the members of the organization see a portion of their job as reminding each other of who they really are. By confirming the innate value in their co-workers, people feel less need to prove themselves better than others. Security is experienced as something other than being the ruler of a small subsystem.

The third role of a leader is to be a *facilitator*. That which facilitates makes something easier. It provides a boost when things are lagging. It instills confidence when things are uncertain. Unlike most images of leadership, which portray it as a relentless action, facilitative leadership comes out of waiting. It is birthed in listening, both without and within. The best facilitation is nurtured from an attitude of acceptance. Ultimately, the facilitator seeks to leave those persons he or she helps better equipped to continue on unassisted. In this sense, facilitative leadership is generative in nature.

Indirect influence is the first characteristic of facilitation. In addition, facilitators have a great concern for conditions. In most situations, the work of the facilitator is not really noticed. As a matter of fact, if the facilitator has done a good job, he or she does very little in the midst of the action. This is so because the facilitator's first responsibility is to help create the conditions that will prevent the system from needing his or her expertise.

Good facilitative leadership understands that to achieve the level of learning which leads to sustainability, organizations need help in defining the attitude of deep learning. Openness, honesty, and unhurried reflection are essential elements of this attitude. In addition to attitude, no system stays healthy without opportunities for connection. The facilitator will ensure that such opportunities exist. Beyond setting in place conditions for learning, the facilitator is constantly trying to limit those conditions that may inhibit the organization's growth.

The second characteristic of facilitation is the art of waiting. Truly, the benefit provided by a facilitator may be only one or two brief moments out of long intervals of interaction in which a choice is clarified. Thus, what could have been a downward spiral is changed into a moment of insight. Waiting to see what emerges is of primary concern to the facilitator. Without such waiting, there is no facilitation, only direction. It is the patience of the facilitator that allows the truly transformative moment to be noticed. The members of the system are too busy solving problems and debating solutions to really wait. The facilitator does this tedious work because it is necessary and few others do it. Most of the time, it is not as glorious as riding in to save the day. When things begin to come apart, the facilitative leader does not rally the troops to continue trying harder. Rather, he or she provides space to wait and see what the next step might be. By slowing down, the way becomes clear. It is a counterintuitive move, to be sure. It is, nonetheless, the source of sustainable transformation.

Conditions and waiting are actualized in facilitation through *listening*. The facilitative leader has attentive ears. He or she listens without and listens within. He or she hears between the words of others in order to create an awareness of things that are said so often that they are, in fact, no longer heard. This listening to others allows the facilitative leader to hold up a mirror to others. When others are too caught up in the proclamation of their own ideas, the facilitative leader listens to the common thread that will bind the diverse points of view into some entirely new story.

Listening within is a different matter. At the same time he or she is listening intently to the process and content of others, the facilitative leader is quite aware of what is occurring within himself or herself. The deeper implication of this inward listening is that the facilitative leader influences others, not by telling them what to do but by being how they should be. To do otherwise is always to be waiting for others to get it. This leaves organizations floundering and their leaders handcuffed. It is also the seed of great division between those leaders who see what is needed and those who do not. Listening within allows a mindset that is not concerned with who does and doesn't get it. What is important is that the facilitative leader can be what is needed to promote sustainability. Others will come along as the vision opens up to them.

Leadership has an essential quality of awareness. Considered in this light, it is reasonable to heed Friedman's insight that leadership is fundamentally an emotional process.[1] It is critical to understand this idea. Leadership is less about being able to get people to do things for you and more about being clear about your beliefs and demonstrating that you are courageous enough to act on them. Leadership is concerned with acting in such a way that the emotional processes (i.e., our natural ability to take in information from the environment and respond to it) are altered so that anxiety no longer paralyzes and creative responses are made possible. In this sense, leadership is primarily concerned with creating an ever greater level of maturity in the system (e.g., the family, team or organization). Namely, those members who exercise leadership become more responsible for themselves rather than others—more connected than distant, more intentional than reactive.

> *I want to stress that by well-differentiated leader I do not mean someone who autocratically tells others what to do or coercively orders them around, although any leader who defines him or herself clearly may be perceived that way by those who are not taking responsibility for their own emotional being and destiny. Rather, I mean someone who has clarity about his or her own life goals, and, therefore, someone who is less likely to become lost in the anxious emotional processes swirling about. I mean someone who can be separate while still remaining connected, and therefore can maintain a modifying, non-anxious, and sometimes challenging presence. I mean someone who can manage his or her own reactivity to the automatic reactivity of others, and therefore be able to take stands at the risk of displeasing.[2]*

Leadership needs to be understood as a function of relationship. Leadership is the ability to influence others and to be influenced. Leaders are most influential when they are focused on self-definition and self-regulation rather than attending to the expectations of others. But, since relationship is the context, the influence of leadership must be reciprocal. Leadership that is intent on changing others is destined to fail. If this seems contradictory, it is. Leadership is most effective when those acting in that capacity realize that their effect on others must be indirect. This indirectness means influencing others by changing yourself and the way you interact in a relationship.[3; 4]

Conclusion

This book defines leadership as the ability to influence the system in such a way that individuals within the system become increasingly more intentional, responsible, mature, and aware. Developing this ability is fundamentally a deep learning process. This way of thinking will allow organizations of all types to quit repeating the past by organizing around mistrust and immaturity. Rather, sustainable organizations continuously seek to organize around trust and maturity. They are constantly learning from experience in order to increase their members' responses in the face of complex situations.

Context

Each of us lives and participates in systems of relationships. Some of those systems possess an atmosphere of fear and anxiety. Others promote conditions of openness, freedom and self-determination. Leadership is one of the few critical levers capable of transforming systems of fear into systems of freedom. If transformational change is to be a real possibility, the first question to be considered is the very nature of the change being pursued. This dialogue thus begins by considering the difference of sustainable change that brings progress versus change that results in sameness. It is this purpose of sustainable change that will be a guide to view the particular characteristics of leadership.

Chapter 2 - Leading In an Age of Change

"An old sage was once walking along a path. . . . Another man . . . approached from the other direction. The young man's eyes were so riveted on the path that he bumped into the sage. The sage looked at the young man sternly, and asked him where he was going. 'To catch my future,' the young man replied. 'How do you know you haven't already passed it?' the sage asked."
Lee Bolman and Terrence Deal - <u>Leading with the Soul</u>

This story describes the similarity of how many individuals, teams, and organizations are swiftly moving along the path to the future. But, during this time of rapid change, many leaders, like the young man in the story, are not paying attention to their surroundings. They are racing ahead towards a 'better' future, but are neglecting to make sure they are headed towards progress.

Much like the sage of the story, effective leaders need to ask a different question: Will this effort of change, of whatever form or fashion, move toward progress or will it lead to sameness? Progress can be thought of in two ways. First, is the change that is occurring really changing anything fundamentally? Is there a real difference? Much of the change that is being pursued today really is changing the appearance and surface form of things but is not fundamentally changing anything.[1]

Second, progress can be thought of in terms of capacity. Is the change that is being pursued and implemented increasing the capacity of individuals within organizations to change more effectively in the future? In a time when organizations are increasingly viewed as living, adaptive systems, there is an increased understanding that change is not an event but a way of being. The only organizations that will endure over time are those that continue to change and adapt. In addition, those organizations and individuals who are capable of participating in change will be most effective.

Again, the question for effective leaders to ask is: Is the change that is being engaged by so many leading to progress or sameness? If change is intentional and chosen, based on a self-defined belief, we will move toward progress. Such change leads to greater maturity and self-responsibility, and creativity is induced. The implication is that self-defined change results from a careful consideration of the assumptions and values that develop from our interactions and worldviews.

On the other hand, change can lead toward regression. Regression is a state of amplified anxiety that generates an ever-decreasing capability to be responsible and to respond creatively. In contrast to an intentional decision, change that is fueled by anxiety will generate much activity, but in the end, there will be only sameness.[2; 3]

Here are a few examples. Family therapists recognize two extreme forms of relationships among family members. On one end of the spectrum, there are families who are enmeshed. These are families in which there is little or no emotional separation between family members. There is no sense of clear boundaries. Members have great difficulty separating thinking and feeling. As a result, there is an unhealthy demand for togetherness. At the other end of the spectrum are families that are said to be cut off. These are families in which members create distance between themselves. This distance is often physical, but it can also be emotional. Family members interact intellectually but are careful to not be emotionally vulnerable. It is important to notice that on the surface, these family dynamics will look and feel very different. However, underlying both extremes are individuals who cannot manage their own anxiety around family relationships. At a deeper level, the extremes are the same. In fact, family members often seek change and behave by moving to the other end of the spectrum, but fundamentally, there is no change.

Let us consider something much different. In the twentieth century, there have been two great political ideologies engaged in a tremendous struggle. On one side is capitalism, an ideology based on competition in free markets. Progress is viewed as growth and is fueled by the entrepreneurial endeavors of those with capital to invest. In the early portion of the twentieth century, this system was plagued by tremendous abuses, as the wealthy used their resources and influence to create monopolies. Workers who were drawn into urban factories were treated as property. In addition, as the new market economies developed, this funded and created motivation for greater imperialism by the industrialized nations.

In response to capitalism, Karl Marx's *Manifesto* became an alternative source for a guiding ideology. In contrast to the industrial barons who hoarded wealth and power, Marxist followers envisioned a society that was owned by the workers. Wealth and power would be distributed more equally. Many nations of Eastern Europe, and particularly the Soviet Union, resented the advancement of the industrialized nations and formed governments based largely on Marxist ideals. The government would own the businesses and resources, thus acting as a regulator to disperse wealth evenly.

One ideology gave rise to the other. Communism developed as a response to a capitalistic system, in which wealth and power were centralized into the hands of a few. Yet in the end, the communistic system developed a much more brutal system, in which wealth and power were again centralized into the hands of a few. Great struggle and sacrifice of resources and lives took place in this political development, but the results were very much the same.

Why? The fundamental assumptions of power, wealth, and governance were never really addressed. Surface changes, driven by ever-escalating reactions to the other side, created fundamentally the same dynamic.

> **Fundamental change is a way of being in which you continuously seek greater ability to be aware of your emotional process, assumptions, and the effectiveness of responses.**

Leaders today run the risk of the very same outcomes. Great effort will be put into changing organizational structures, business strategies, and organizational cultures. However, if no one questions the nature of those changes, the past will only be re-created in a different form. For instance, the great promise of freedom and empowerment of the Internet may simply result in different individuals gathering wealth and power. Leaders need to consider that change for progress requires them to think about the nature of their interactions, the nature of the pursuit of change, and their paradigms for how change is sustained. These three ideas will form the context for the following discussion as to the nature of leadership that results in continuous, sustainable change. The learning model, illustrated in Figure 3.1, can act as a road map for all levels of systems involved in creating this change. If tomorrow is truly to improve on yesterday, it will be necessary to look deep within to discover what about human nature has created systems that ultimately do not work.

Fundamental change is not an event. It is a process. It is a way of being in which you continuously seek greater ability to be aware of your emotional process, assumptions, and the effectiveness of responses. In this sense, fundamental change can be considered learning. This model provides a way of seeing yourself and the dynamics of the system, which then informs direction for real, sustainable change. This process of seeing yourself and the dynamics of the system is not a destination, event, or answer to be obtained. It is an ongoing process that requires constant attention, lest leaders fall back into automated ways of thinking and acting. It involves a continual adjustment of how we see ourselves, other people, and the world in which we all live. We will need to unlearn as many things as we will learn. Leaders will be called to let go of the deeply learned actions to avoid embarrassment or failure.

Successful leaders do not attempt to change others; rather, they change themselves. They look within and understand the fear-based models that too often guide their behavior. They risk the fear of embarrassment or failure in order to pursue the more noble course of honesty, courage and truth. Such insight allows different kinds of human interaction to emerge. Additionally, it alters the nature of our change efforts altogether. No longer will we seek to force some condition or mindset upon others, but we will seek to influence others intentionally by clearly defining our own selves and creating conditions for others to do the same. In this way, change comes to be seen as an ongoing process of learning. We challenge the assumptions that forge our fearful reactions. We let go of many things that inhibit the conditions of openness so imperative for learning. In so doing, we have a greater chance of creating change that leads to progress rather than reinventing a failed form of the past. Like the young man in the story at the beginning of this chapter, how will you know if you are headed towards progress? By being aware of your surroundings and persistently asking if the change being pursued is leading to progress or to sameness.

An Adventurous Society

Too often individuals pursue change only to re-create in another form what it was that motivated the change in the first place. As an example, this chapter will end with the story of a nation that seems to have understood something of this idea. Ending decades of oppression, South Africa was faced with at least two choices. Its citizens could exchange oppression of the minority for oppression of the majority, or they could attempt to create something quite different from their past. For this example these choices have been oversimplified, for there was much at risk. If the leaders on both sides of this political movement made decisions based on fear, they would inevitably re-create some form of oppression.

Although at times, the current circumstances in South Africa may seem bleak (i.e., a country with a horrid history on a developing continent), this nation can be held up as an experiment in progress. The jury is still out as to how successful its endeavor will be. Nonetheless, South Africa offers a courageous story of leaders and a society that seeks progress over comfort. Out of decades of oppression, the Truth and Reconciliation Commission emerged as an adventurous attempt to heal a fragmented society.

> *April 27, 1994, the watershed date, the beginning of a new era, ushered in the new South Africa, the democratic nonracial, nonsexist South Africa of the election slogans. That was something quite novel—a democracy in place of the repression and injustice of the old discredited apartheid. We were very soon to discover that almost nobody really would now admit to having supported this vicious system. Something new had to come into existence on April 27.* [4]

This remarkable event was a crossroads for an entire nation. One way would replicate the same repressive mindset but with different players on top. The other way promised long-term sustainability but with a great deal of short-term discomfort. On one path, the transfer of power would surely lead to a bloodbath as the majority government took power. The other path, the one less traveled, offered a nonviolent transfer of power. One path seemed natural for a people decimated by prejudice. The other path seemed illogical and counterintuitive but contained the necessary elements for starting something new on April 27, 1994.

The world is a great deal more fortunate because the leaders on both sides did not bow to the perceived threat of discomfort and chose instead a path to healing. This story of courageous leadership should be seen not as a method to duplicate but as an example to learn from. It would not seem possible to find a more emotionally laden system than that of South Africa emerging from apartheid. Yet the self-differentiated leadership offered by both F. W. de Klerk and Nelson Mandela has offered the hope of real healing for this tattered nation. De Klerk faced the potential wrath of his own minority government and the pent-up hatred of people who had been oppressed for over thirty years. He chose to seek progress over comfort. "Nothing will ever take away from F. W. de Klerk the enormous credit that belongs to him for what he said and did then. He has carved out a niche for himself in the history of South Africa and, whatever his reasons for doing so and whatever our assessment of what he did subsequently, we should salute him for what he did in 1990."[5] Rather than protect his own position at all costs, de Klerk took a critical first step in opening the door to reform.

His gesture of courage would have been for naught had he not found a man of noble character on the other side. After having been imprisoned for over twenty years, Nelson Mandela could have created a dire situation had he been unwilling to let go of his need to blame and seek revenge. "Had F.

W. de Klerk encountered in jail a man bristling with bitterness and a lust for retribution, it is highly unlikely that he would have gone ahead with announcing his initiatives."[6] What de Klerk did encounter was a man who put the health of the nation before his own validation. Not yielding to the threat of eruption among his own people, Mandela and de Klerk negotiated a path to peace. The form of this path was the Truth and Reconciliation Commission.

The Truth and Reconciliation Commission was an amendment to the interim constitution of the new South Africa. According to the Promotion of National Unity and Reconciliation Act of 1995, the commission had seven prescribed tasks:

1. *To provide for the investigation and establishment of as complete a picture as possible, of the nature, causes and extent of gross violations of human rights, committed from 1960 until the 10th of May 1994 when President Mandela was inaugurated. So to provide as complete a picture as possible of what happened both inside South Africa and outside.*

2. *To ascertain the fate or whereabouts of the victims of such violations.*

3. *The granting of amnesty to persons who made full disclosure, that is, of all acts associated with the political objective committed in the course of the conflicts of the past.*

4. *Affording victims an opportunity to relate the violations they suffered.*

5. *The taking of measures aimed at granting reparation to, and the rehabilitation and the restoration of the human and civil dignity of victims.*

6. *Reporting to the nation about such violations and victims.*

7. *The making of recommendations aimed at the prevention of the commission of gross violations in the future.*[7]

Beyond any of the specific strategy outlined in the charter for the Commission, the nature of such an action bears the characteristics of a mature and adventurous society that sought real and creative solutions to difficult circumstances. This story can reveal some of what is needed if a sustainable system—whether a family, team, organization, or society—is the desired result. Specifically, the characteristics demonstrated were a telling of the truth, an increase in the knowledge of that truth by all, differentiated leadership, and a promotion of personal responsibility and patience.

Any hope of substantial change had to include telling the truth. In fact, rather than simply taking revenge on the oppressors, Mandela's government understood that something more profound was needed. Just granting amnesty for political favor would be unacceptable as would allowing the oppressed to become the oppressors. Amnesty would be granted in exchange for two things: responsibility and truth. In fact, amnesty had to be applied for and would only result in exchange for full disclosure. Secrets create division, which increases anxiety. It should be noted that it is not so much the content of the secrets but the act of keeping secrets, of covering up, which perpetuates dysfunction. South Africa would have absolutely no chance of significant change without truth rising to the surface.

Telling the truth as a course of action was a risky choice. What would happen when all the horrid details began to surface? Would the collective anger of a people oppressed for over thirty years rage out of control? Could the perpetrators hope to have any life at all after the truth came out? Questions such as these posed a crossroads for the people of South Africa. The leadership chose health over comfort and took the risk of providing complete disclosure. The truth telling was not done in quiet, darkened backrooms with only a few to hear. The Truth and Reconciliation Commission was a public entity and hearings were held in the open. Moreover, the results and recommendations of the Commission were a matter of public record. It is important to point out: Politicians did not just deposit the report in a place with such limited access that only a legal insider would know where to find it. Truth telling was genuine and sincere, as demonstrated by making the public record open to everyone through mass media and other organizations such as The Center for the Study of Violence and Reconciliation, which provided some follow-up to the Commission hearings.

> *Truth is always a path to health. It is not always easy or comfortable, but it is the only basis for any real trust.*

Truth is always a path to health. It is not always easy or comfortable, but it is the only basis for any real trust. It provides redemption for imperfect people. It not only guards against those who seek personal gain at the expense of others, but it also provides protection against our own fears. "By uncovering lies and official misconduct, which form the cornerstone of the abuse of power, truth commissions aim to lay the foundation for the reestablishment of the rule of law. Truth has a democratizing effect because it is more difficult to sustain arbitrary and repressive rule in a society comprised of citizens who know the terrible costs of human rights abuse."[8]

The effect of truth telling and allowing all to participate in such truth telling is that it creates the conditions for the more mature to rise to the top. Failing to tell the truth for fear of embarrassment or reprisal would keep the system in the hands of the least mature. The choice of South Africa allowed the best people to come forward. Rather than produce a bloodbath, the truth commissions produced examples of tremendous human capacity for dignity and honor. Individuals on both sides demonstrated great courage, as many came to realize that abuse of human rights dehumanizes everyone.

What was truly remarkable about the response of the South African people was that the truth commissions were not used as a tool of blame and reversed oppression. When the truth is being told with sincerity, it creates an awareness of everyone's participation in the system. In the Commission hearings, many of the black community stood up and took responsibility for their part. The following example demonstrated the great courage and humanity possible:

Just before midnight, a small group of young people, all black, in their twenties, came with an application for amnesty. They asked for amnesty "for apathy."

In applying for amnesty for apathy the persons here recognize the following:

1. *That we individuals can and should be held accountable by history for our lack of necessary action in times of crisis.*
2. *That none of us did all of what we could have done to make a difference in the anti-apartheid struggle.*
3. *That in exercising apathy rather than commitment, we allowed others to sacrifice their lives for the sake of our freedom and an increase in our standard of living.*
4. *That apathy is a real and powerful phenomenon and perhaps the most destructive one in society.*
5. *That society takes a leap forward when individuals hold themselves accountable for their lack of action commensurate with change that needs to be made.*[9]

These are not lone or isolated examples of the responses to the testimony during the hearings. Ordinary people became great in their individual moments of truth and forgiveness. Too often, such courage is not allowed to surface because of the fear of what might be. Leaders, who take the easy way out, have meetings only with other leaders who will not hold each other accountable. To do so would break an often unwritten code. When communication does go out, it is also apparent that it is a spin on the truth. This only deepens the grip that fear and cynicism have on an organization. True healing and sustainability are not possible.

The greatest gift from the leaders of South Africa is that they chose to trust their people rather than seek their own comfort. The result was an array of amazing acts of humanity. Differentiated leaders are capable of such acts, for they are guided by things other than fear and comfort. Differentiated leaders pursue the truth, maturity, and responsibility. They do so first themselves and thus create the possibility that others can and will follow.

It would be untrue to give the impression that everything today is better in South Africa. It is not. Although critically important, the Truth and Reconciliation Commission was not perfect and has not exacted complete healing.[10] There is still much to be done. Hard work is still required for a full healing of South Africa. However, nonreactive, differentiated systems do not require quick fixes. Such things do not exist. Sustainable health will result only from continued efforts, such as the one that produced the Commission. Patience is imperative for sustainable change.

Conclusion

We all can begin to understand that the organizations and societies that we live in are created by our choices. Waiting for someone else to come in and fix things can no longer be acceptable. Each of us contributes to the creation and sustainability of the systems that we find ourselves inhabiting. The only hope that those systems can move beyond fear to a place of freedom is for all individuals to take the responsibility to change themselves. This is the fundamental thought of this book – Leaders who create the healthiest systems realize that their greatest source of influence is not in forcing others to change but in changing themselves.

Theory

The emerging roles for leaders require a particular fortitude, mindset, and character. The next chapter introduces a model for understanding the profound learning leaders will require in the future. Only persistent practice will yield leaders of noble character, able to call others to their highest potential.

Chapter 3 - The Learning Dynamic of Differentiation

"I shall be telling this with a sigh
somewhere ages and ages hence:
Two roads diverged in a wood, and I—
I took the one less traveled by,
And that has made all the difference."
Robert Frost - <u>The Road Not Taken</u>

Leaders, when all is said and done, do at least two things. First, they dare to lift the curtain and help us look beyond the illusions that confine us. They loan us a bit of imagination as they fan the ember of hope that lies anxiously awaiting to ignite within us. We have all tasted this briefly—somewhere, somehow—the freedom that is found in authenticity. It usually comes as a wisp. Out of the corner of your eye, you catch a movement. Your head turns, and when you look back, the illumination is gone, leaving only a nagging suspicion that something more profound does exist. From then on, you will never be satisfied until you experience that freedom again.

The second thing that leaders do is to dare to look first and be the first to step onto the path that leads to progress. Freedom requires that we let go in order to hang on. Natural cycles teach us that life comes out of death. Those who hang onto security, certainty, and control will never be able to see beyond their self-imposed constraints. Due to upbringing, experience, or fate, leaders become aware first and are not contained by the fear of taking the first step toward a new way.

The age we live in is calling for such people. The question is how to become such a leader. How can you start along the path to greater awareness, freedom, and purposeful choice? This chapter will provide a model that suggests how to do so. The emerging roles for leaders require a particular fortitude, mindset and character. This model of differentiated learning describes an ongoing process that will guide leaders as they continue to mature in character. The model's purpose is to help reveal the dynamics involved in learning, changing, and self-differentiation.

Leadership is comprised of more than traits, behaviors, and roles. It goes beyond the technique aimed at getting others to do what you want them to do. It is a process for considering and empowering those in the leader's sphere of influence. It is an ongoing process of becoming more and more aware and vigilant. It is a position of watching that seeks to be conscious of the corrupting nature of power, whether used or not. It is taking a sentinel stance to be on alert for situations, circumstances, people, and practices that amplify anxiety in the systems they lead. It is to understand the emotional process of the system—to acknowledge the automatic behavior driven by the need to find immediate comfort in the face of difficult circumstances. This is a process of continuously seeking to know yourself, to clarify your thinking, to take responsibility rather than place blame, and to control only yourself. In doing so, the conditions will be set for others to follow in their own journey towards differentiation. Leaders who are more differentiated understand what it takes for a person to uncover and challenge assumptions as well as limit automatic, anxiety driven responses in order to be more intentional. The mere presence of a leader who is not reactive, will dissipate the anxiety of the group and allow them to begin to consider new ways of understanding the situation and themselves. Just as important as what the leader does is what a differentiated leader will not do. He or she will not rescue individuals in order to restore peace. Neither will he or she manipulate others to comply by asserting their position or providing only part of the information. When a critical mass of any organization can practice such leadership, the anxious gridlock will be loosened and a creative, sustainable, adventurous spirit will emerge.

Knowing yourself is no small undertaking. It should not be taken lightly. This endeavor will require great courage, as you see both the potential and the limitations that reside within. Most people do not choose this path. Rather, they rely on position and the illusionary power that comes with position. Those who want to have a profound and generative impact on their sphere of influence must be willing to recognize that awareness, courage, and influence are gifts that must be applied for the betterment of the whole. Those who realize what real leadership is often are hesitant. Their caution comes from a deep awareness that leadership and influence are not trivial matters to be manipulated for personal satisfaction.

The following passage from *The Scions of Shannara*, a Terry Brooks novel, reveals the nature of courageous intention necessary for leadership:

> *"You believe we might be the ones for whom the trust was intended. . . . I believe it—and I am frightened by the possibility as I have never been frightened of anything in my life!" Walker's voice was a low hiss. "I am terrified of it! I want no part of the Druids and their mysteries! I want nothing to do with the Elven magic, with its demands and its treacheries! I wish only to be left alone, to live out my life in a way I believe useful and fulfilling—and that is all I wish!" Par let his eyes drop protectively against the fury of the other man's words. Then he smiled sadly. "Sometimes the choice isn't ours, Walker." Walker's reply was unexpected. "That was what I decided." His lean face was hard as Par looked up again. "While I waited for you to wake, while I kept myself apart from the others, out there in the forests beyond Storlock, that was what I decided." He shook his head. "Events and circumstances sometimes conspire against us; if we insist on inflexibility for the purpose of maintaining our beliefs, we end up compromising ourselves nonetheless. We salvage one set of principles only to forsake another."* [1]

The first step toward responsible leadership is to develop a clear sense of self. Developing a sense of self is an on going process of learning, changing and reframing your view of yourself in relation to the rest of the world. Only then will you possess the clarity and character to promote maturity and health in others.

A Picture of Differentiation

A way for a leader to develop a clear sense of self is to learn to pay attention to the dynamic involved with the interactions around them. We have developed a model that provides a language for this process. It is both a picture of the underlying dynamic involved in learning, change, and differentiation and a description of the core abilities needed to see the path and head down it. This model is based on the work of Peck,[2] and Wheatley and Kellner-Rogers.[3]

In essence, the dynamic is so fundamental because it is consistent with the natural rhythms of life. Each life grows out of some previous death, and each death produces the next life. In addition, the dynamic is surrounded by four core learning abilities that allow a person to participate in and cooperate with the dynamic rather than fight or deny it (see Figure 3.1).

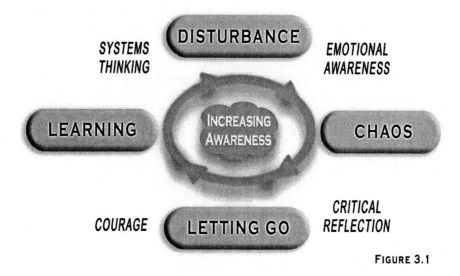

SYSTEMS
THINKING

DISTURBANCE

EMOTIONAL
AWARENESS

LEARNING

INCREASING
AWARENESS

CHAOS

COURAGE

LETTING GO

CRITICAL
REFLECTION

FIGURE 3.1

As a way to make this theory more practical, we will use the story of Phil Jackson and his success with the Chicago Bulls and Los Angeles Lakers as an example of a leader who experienced dramatic success. At first glance, using Jackson as an example for leaders may seem a bit trivial. In the broader scope of political, military, religious and business leaders, a basketball coach may not seem to measure up in credibility. However, models for successful leadership in the future will not be found in the mainstream. Rather, it will be those on the fringe that may pave the path for others to follow.

In many ways, the role of the professional basketball coach is similar to any other high profile leadership position. Phil Jackson faced the well-recognized pressure of a tight labor pool, where recruiting and retaining the best talent is imperative. He was the most recognized leader in a multibillion-dollar industry. He managed a multimillion-dollar payroll. In addition, the competitive advantage for a team is the consistent execution of a well-defined strategy. There are three more reasons why Phil Jackson is a good example to use. First, his success not only took him to the top of his profession, but his success was sustainable. His teams won nine of the last fourteen NBA championships, a feat that is surpassed only by the run of the Boston Celtics in the 1950's and 1960's. Second, he was able to yield such results not with one team but with three different teams. His leadership was demonstrated to be transferable. He was not just lucky. He had to form and reform multiple teams. Third, in an age when the mechanistic, command and control paradigm of organizations is breaking down and giving way to a model that views organizations as living, complex systems where all members are participating and continually adapting, Jackson's teams were models of this new way of business. Not only did Jackson treat his players with great respect and dignity, he sought to develop their entire person - mind, body and spirit. In addition, his offensive scheme was a radical departure of traditional style offense. It is not just that he ran different formations; his offense reflected his deep commitment to the notion that all players are valued members of the team and each is able and responsible to make significant contributions. He was able to demonstrate that by teaching all members how to be self-sustaining, the team was stronger not weaker. Information is not confined to a few, for in his scheme all were taught not only to understand information that is given but how to create their own knowledge by evaluating what is occurring in the environment in which they are working.

Disturbance

Disturbance is the first phase of the learning model. All significant learning begins with a Disturbance. The Disturbance can be external, such as a change in market conditions, a new mandate from above, a stretch goal to reduce cost and increase revenue, or a child turning thirteen. Consider the mother bird that insistently crowds her offspring to the edge of the nest in order to force them into the awareness that birds fly. Or it can be an internal stirring of restlessness with the status quo. Regardless of its origin, the Disturbance begins a new cycle of learning and change. In the beginning, a person may only be slightly aware that something new has begun.

There is no guarantee that every Disturbance will lead to learning. It is possible—through years of not paying attention or insensitivity due to fear or busyness—not to notice that something in the internal or external environment is signaling that change needs to occur. Often, the Disturbance is ignored intentionally with the hope that by not giving heed, it will go away. Along with the strategies for quickly relieving the next phase of Chaos, this inattention often paralyzes the learning process. In reality, a Disturbance that is ignored will only return in a much louder form.

An Example of Disturbance

In 1989, Phil Jackson was named the head coach of the Chicago Bulls. He entered this role with a vision of what it would take to make the team into a high performing team. His vision was very different from any other coach in the league. He describes his intent this way:

The day I took over the Bulls, I vowed to create an environment based on the principles of selflessness and compassion I'd learned as a Christian in my parents' home; sitting on a cushion practicing Zen; and studying the teachings of the Lakota Sioux. I knew that the only way to win consistently was to give everybody—from the stars to the number 12 player on the bench—a vital role on the team, and inspire them to be acutely aware of what was happening, even when the spotlight was on somebody else. More than anything, I wanted to build a team that would blend talent with a heightened group consciousness. A team that could win big without becoming small in the process.[4]

In order to make this vision a reality, Jackson had to begin to disturb the system. He did this through his mannerisms, presence and philosophy. But the loudest Disturbance came when he changed the offensive scheme and consequently changed the role of the greatest player of the game—Michael Jordan. The institution of the triangle offense asked Jordan to believe that he could accomplish more with less. Rather than being the focal point, the triangle offense made all five players on the court a threat. However, it would require Jordan to trust his teammates and take fewer shots.

Chaos

Once there is awareness that something is beginning to take shape, a period of uncertainty will most likely be experienced. This uncertainty signals the beginning of the second phase of the learning model called Chaos. It is the discomfort that comes when you know that change is necessary but the new vision has not yet become clear. Depending on the perceived intensity of the learning process, Chaos may be no more than a momentary hesitation while you gather yourself and establish a new sense of direction. On the other hand, Chaos may approach what is often described as "a dark night of the soul." These moments of self-searching can provide the springboard to an entirely new way of seeing yourself in the world.

As with Disturbance, the experience of Chaos does not always lead to change. For many, the messiness of the Chaos phase is too threatening. An automatic, reactive response to such an experience is to relieve the immediate discomfort. Those seeking quick relief are hoping for a leader to come and make things right. In the absence of such a hero, they will also blame those who do not rescue them. Often, this is the place at which leaders become sidetracked in their role. Leaders can become overly sensitive to their own or others' discomfort and eliminate the hope of lasting change in exchange for enjoying momentary relief. Progress will not be made, however, if feeling comfortable takes precedence over developing maturity and growth.

An Example of Chaos

Phil Jackson brought to the Bulls a new vision, a new structure and new processes. As he implemented his strategy, there were times of Chaos. Players were uncertain and confused. If Jackson had not possessed faith, confidence and most importantly determination, he would have not realized his vision. Like all change, there were moments of Chaos that challenged the new way. Jordan describes it like this:

> *In the beginning I fought the triangle. I thought Phil believed all the talk about not being able to win a championship with me leading the league in scoring. I thought he went to the offense to take the ball out of my hands. For the first time since college, I wasn't the first option. The first option was to throw the ball inside to either Horace (Grant) or Bill (Cartwright). I wasn't alone in fighting the system. Everyone hated it in the beginning because it was so difficult to operate. But Phil never backed off.*[5]

Letting Go

Letting Go is the most critical work in the entire process and the third phase in the learning model. Disturbance will come and go without consent, and Chaos will emerge from unawareness. But Letting Go involves making a choice. Letting Go does not mean that we can or should throw away experience, ideas, preferences, or assumptions. Letting Go is a loosening of the grip we hold on certain things. The failure to loosen the grip and consider the possibilities of new perspectives will result in a tyranny of the Chaos from which you are seeking refuge. Learning occurs in an open space in which listening and being influenced are freely chosen. Isaacs captures the essence of this well when he says, "It is the ability to let go, to 'suspend' our certainty, the rigid opinion we may have formed about something, to see things from another point of view."[6]

Letting Go is the first step in being intentional about what we think and the actions those thoughts generate. It is fundamentally more of an emotional process than a cognitive one. Thinking and feeling are no longer allowed to be fused. What you feel is not necessarily reality. Letting Go is refusing to let fear determine who you are. It is not the answer, but it sets the stage for finding more answers, both individually and collectively.

Since Letting Go is the decisive step between never-ending spirals of Chaos and Learning, growth, and maturity, it is important to understand exactly *what* a person is letting go of. Although this list is not exhaustive, learning is served when we are able to let go of our comfort, our certainty, and our need for control.

As an emotional process, Letting Go is a willingness to give up the need for comfort in order to be open to something new. The need for comfort is the primary precursor to a regressive, anxious system. This need for comfort creates a quick-fix mentality. Those who cannot or will not endure discomfort long enough to learn and take responsibility for their lives will choose to believe in a "magical answer"—a solution that will bring immediate relief without the requisite work of learning and choosing for themselves. This belief keeps systems at all levels (i.e., individuals, teams, and organizations) focused on "technological and administrative solutions."[7] With that as the focus, learning will be impossible. There will never be enough patience in the system to wrestle with complex issues.

Closely related to the need for comfort is the need for certainty, which could also be thought of as the need to be right. Again, Learning is about slowing down and reflecting on successes and failures in order to create a deeper sense of the meaning of the world around us. This cannot happen when you are focused on being right. Finally, there is the need for control. What makes this a poisonous element is that the need for control is never just about taking responsibility for yourself; instead, it is the illusion that a person can and should control the environment, all circumstances, and all the people who make up their world. As the attempts to control or form others in your own image increase, so does the amount of reactivity and anxiety in the system. Learning will not occur in such violent conditions. On a deeper level, it is apparent that the need to control others is an attempt to somehow heal yourself by fixing others. The emptiness that people experience and their basic mistrust of their own value make them depend on others for validation. Often, they expect that validation to be revealed by others agreeing with them, following their cue as to what is right and wrong and seeing things as they see things. An example of this need for comfort, certainty and control showed up in a recent training program. A potential trainer was invited to observe a two-day portion of a certification program. There was a very talented and competent instructor facilitating the class, but the potential trainer had such a need for comfort, certainty and control that she challenged, argued, and attacked the facilitator and the content of the training throughout the entire first day. Realizing this woman had special needs, the facilitator talked privately with her at lunch and at the end of the first day. The facilitator's hope was to gain her as an ally for the second day, but talking didn't help. The woman continued her behavior throughout the

> *As an emotional process, Letting Go is a willingness to give up the need for comfort in order to be open to something new.*

second day. She had such a need for others to agree with her that the program was bad and to validate her as the 'expert'. Her need to be right blinded her to any other potential perspectives on the subject. This also illustrates another telltale sign that this issue was more an emotional one than an intellectual one. People driven by their anxiety do not learn from their experience. No amount of reasoning, information or technique works to redirect such a person. The only driver they respond to is the need to be comfortable, certain and in control.

This is how the need for comfort, certainty, and control becomes a deeply inhibiting force, keeping learning at bay. If I need others to validate me, I cannot move on until I convince them that I am right. This is a dead-end road because I am not focusing on myself but on changing them. Peck identifies healing and converting as a perceived quick fix out of Chaos.[8] I cannot feel good about myself until someone else feels good about me. Letting Go of all this illusion will allow me to enter a place of space in which there is a feel of openness. I do not require others to be like me but only that they become more clear themselves. This is an atmosphere more akin to hospitality.

> *Hospitality, therefore, means primarily the creating of a free space where a team member can enter and become a friend instead of an enemy. Hospitality is not to change people, but to offer them space where change can take place. It is not to bring men and women over to our side, but to offer freedom not disturbed by dividing lines. It is not an educated intimidation with good books, good stories and good works, but the liberation of fearful hearts so that words can find roots and bear ample fruit. It is not a method of making . . . our way into the criteria of success, but opening of an opportunity to others to find their own way.[9]*

An Example of Letting Go

Every leader has those moments where the decision is either to Let Go and empower and mature the organization or to use their position to maintain their own security. Phil Jackson was no different. He implemented his system and began the long process of changing the way the players thought about themselves, each other and the team. Yet had he not had the courage to live what he believed, he would have become just another patriarchal leader. In 1994, a rift emerged between Horace Grant, the Bull's starting forward, and the rest of the team. Horace had decided to play out his option and consider free agency at the end of the year. As the year progressed, Jackson sensed Horace pulling away from the team. Horace, in an attempt to protect the financial opportunity coming to him in free agency, allowed small injuries to keep him from playing. Jackson saw this as betrayal and his anger was fueled.

Jackson had come to a decision point. Would he use his power to coerce or live consistent with the values he was building the organization upon? Jackson describes the outcome this way:

Talking it over with my wife, I realized that my own agenda for Horace was getting in the way of seeing the situation clearly. When I stepped back, I saw how much I blamed Horace for trying to sabotage the season when all he was doing was looking out for his future. What I needed to do was open my heart and try to understand the situation from his point of view. I needed to practice the same selflessness and compassion with Horace that I expected from him on the court. When I was able to relax the steel grip on my heart and finally see him through a less self-centered lens, our relationship was repaired.[10]

Learning

The last phase of the model is Learning which must be understood as something other than accumulating and assimilating new information. Learning is taking the necessary steps to reclaim your identity. No longer will you allow fear to define who you are. This type of change leads people to understand their true sources of value. At its core, this kind of Learning is concerned with three characteristics: awareness, intentionality, and increased coherence. These terms infer the attitude that is necessary for Learning. They also speak to what exactly you are trying to change—to learn and unlearn. This process of continuous change and learning is what ultimately leads to health and sustainability. Consequently, when critical masses of individuals are capable of practicing this type of learning, a system will arise based on freedom rather than fear.

Learning can be thought of as an act of awakening. Awareness begins with clarity around the assumptions that result in decisions made and actions taken. It is only with this level of thinking that new possibilities can arise. Without such awareness, new practices will only be different forms of the same old ones. Or worse, existing practices will continue, guided by automatic and unconscious strategies. Awareness of assumptions—both individual and collective—leads to gaining a more complete picture of what is and greater clarity about what might be.

Waking up is important but not enough. Becoming attentive to what is and what might be has value only if this insight leads to action. As people become more aware, they can be more purposeful with their actions. In this sense, intentionality increases. Intentionality is both an increased sense of choice and a decreased level of reactivity.

The idea of intentionality may seem out of place in a discussion of Learning. However, unless an individual, a group, an organization, or a society develops a mature understanding of the choices available to them, they will continue to point fingers, lay blame, make excuses, and commit a myriad of other behaviors that stifle their ability to change. The principle of intentionality simply refers to Learning as seeing your own contribution to the process and taking responsibility to change yourself in order to influence the system. This is a freeing realization that there are certainly more options for action than are initially apparent. Learners seek to gain a broader perspective on the choices available and the choices made. Such insight empowers the ability to create.

> *The principle of intentionality simply refers to Learning as seeing your own contribution to the process and taking responsibility to change yourself in order to influence the system.*

Here is an example: The secondary effect of increased intentionality is a reduction of reactivity in the system. *Reactivity* refers to the automatic responses that systems (whether individuals, teams, families, or organizations) make in the face of increased anxiety. These responses are impulsive attempts to regain some level of comfort. They are almost always the least effective and least creative responses individuals can make. The irony of the situation is that during crisis - the time when the most effective and creative responses are necessary - the system is least capable of making those types of responses. Instead, there is a hypersensitivity to anything that might be perceived as hurtful. Systems that are highly reactive do not learn from their experience and ultimately become stuck, unable to see their way clear to a better future.[11] Consider for example the current political atmosphere in our country. Too many news shows broadcast arguments cleverly hidden as panel discussions that do little to seek new understanding that might lead to progress. Instead, all that the participants can see are the aspiring goals of their party to be in control. New and creative solutions to longstanding problems cannot emerge in an atmosphere where true listening does not occur. True listening cannot occur until differences are used as strengths, diversity of perspective fuels true curiosity and the critical mass of leaders intentionally place the good of others ahead of their own self-interest and the interest of their parties.

Intentionality reduces reactivity in systems because it changes the focus of the members away from others. Attempts to control or will others to be a certain way always increases the anxiety in a system. Regardless of whether the suggested changes are good, seeking to dominate others will result in a reaction to reestablish individuality or will decrease another's capability to be responsible for himself or herself. Learning that leads to greater insight of choice ends the cycle of resistance and reactivity that keeps individuals from creating positive change. It is amazing how potentially volatile issues can be broached and resolved in an atmosphere of intentionality. Intentionality acts as a pressure-relief valve. Individuals do not have to fear one another's perspectives because they can trust that together they are trying to help each other see all the options available. At the same time, they hold deep respect for one another's need to make their own choices.

Awareness and intentionality finally result in an increased coherence, which is the third characteristic of Learning. Coherence is the understanding that each individual's action occurs in the context of a larger meaning. The parts of the system can be understood in their relationship to the whole. For the individual, this means there is a greater degree of authenticity. Collectively, coherence comes from making meaning of experience.

Coherence begins to emerge as individuals discover that their lives have meaning beyond that which is most obvious. People need to connect to something larger than themselves. With such insight comes an understanding of the true source of your own power. Most of what passes for power is fueled by illusion. The belief that your value comes from your possessions, position, or competence grows from an identity that does not know who you are. Rather, there is the nagging suspicion that something is missing—that your life will have meaning if you can accomplish, accumulate, or acquire that one thing. The acceptance that we all have value releases us from trying to gain through effort what can only be accepted as free. Anything short of such faith leaves us grasping to take from others what already lies within. Coherence is an act of faith. The result is a sense of meaning.

Faith in our intrinsic value, a gift given at our creation, is the foundation of a greater authenticity. Authenticity is the decision to live no longer divided. Authenticity begins when you become truly honest about your entire nature, the light and the shadow. It is manifested when the life that you live is consistent with your identity.

I was once working with a small group of employees in an ongoing leadership development setting. On this particular day, a very energetic and happy young lady became the focus of attention. She tended to be reluctant to talk about herself. So this day's conversation was all the more surprising. She began to talk of how happy she was in her job yet she also talked at length about working long hours. Something in her story seemed inconsistent to me. As I pressed her a bit by asking a few probing questions, she began, through her tears, to divulge how fearful she was of failure. Her over-achieving work habits were really a coping mechanism for a personal shadow that feared failure and was really unsure of her place in the company and in life in general. Since my relationship with this young lady was brief, I do not know what the long term impact of that conversation has had on her. I do know she discovered something that day of the first step towards authenticity.

The first step in authentic living is to tell the truth. Learning is "truly transformative when we start telling the truth to one another, including our mistakes, including our confusion".[12] On the contrary, the fear of having our limitations exposed keeps us separated, fragmented both internally and collectively. The fear of embarrassment or failure turns organizations into dances of dysfunctional acceptance. Such organizations spawn individuals torn between being who they really are and projecting personas of who others want them to be. How many times in school were you afraid to ask a question for fear of appearing dumb? How many good questions do not get asked in organizations because of fear?

> **Learning that heightens awareness, promotes intentionality, and increases coherence allows people to embrace their true selves.**

Learning that heightens awareness, promotes intentionality, and increases coherence allows people to embrace their true selves. A trust can blossom from an understanding that people are more alike than different. Such recognition opens up individuals to pursue the search for meaning together. And that shared understanding may transform into a shared vision. A shared vision will produce organizations in which congruence is the norm.

Shared understanding, shared vision, and shared ownership come from shared experience. When experience is frequently the focus of critical reflection, a common mindset can emerge. Sharing stories and thinking together about the lessons of experience allows not only for the cross-pollination of perspectives but creates the possibility that a new logic can emerge. When individuals, teams, families, or organizations begin to see the world differently, sustainable change is sure to follow. Change occurs when old behaviors no longer make sense. People learn to notice different things and to give new meaning to what they do see.

Conclusion

This brings the discussion full circle to a whole new set of Disturbances that set in motion a new learning adventure. Stability is the paradoxical result of continual change. Learning promotes maturity. Maturity begets responsibility. Responsibility reveals choice. Choice is freedom—one based not on fear but on faith and acceptance. Leaders will find it easier to lead and followers will find it easier to follow in a place such as this.

Application

In the next chapter, one of the authors reveals the utility of the learning model from the inside out. His personal account of real struggles to possess self-differentiated leadership forms the basis of the story. It includes snapshots taken from a journal covering about a two-year time frame. Although they are not complete, they are examples of the questions asked and the experiences had during the pursuit of differentiation. Differentiation is a maturing of your sense of identity that you may have to end up at a different place.

Though his life processes are unique, the workings of the process within him provide some glimpse of how the model can be used. The goal is to show the breadth of the model and that the implications are not just in your work environment but can stretch into all areas of your life.

Chapter 4 - A Personal Quest of Differentiation

"...courage ... is not to conquer others but to conquer yourself."
Peter Koestenbaum — <u>The Inner Side of Greatness</u>

My first professional position was with a small Baptist church in northwest Arkansas. I was nineteen years old when I was named junior high director/janitor. It was a dream come true for a naïve youth, full of idealism and inspiration. Although I was paid to mop floors, my heart was with the kids. I was successful by all the measures this church used to define success. The group had nearly tripled in size during my term as director and the youth genuinely cared for their church, their faith, and each other.

After nearly two years, a wave of reality washed me away as I stood in the pastor's office, listening to him tell me I was no longer wanted. The cause of the dismissal was his insecurity. I know this to be true because he accused the entire staff of wanting his job. Subsequently, all staff members—from secretary to associate minister—were released within the year. Shell shocked, I limped back home, not really knowing what had happened. This institution was not supposed to be this way. My anger burned deep as I saw for the first time the dysfunction of human organizations.

I experienced some variation of this story several more times in my ten-year career as a youth minister, including a particularly painful variation of this cycle during a four-year stint with a Christian university. After having created a new program from nothing, I was maneuvered out of my position. The reason for my leaving was that I was on the wrong side of an internal feud of ideologies.

The stories were different, but the message was the same. Changing the system would not be tolerated, no matter how successful the program might be. I grew in wisdom as well as cynicism. I learned to play the game better, but I was not really able to make much sense of it all until several years later.

Nearly fifteen years after my first rejection, I found myself working in corporate America. I watched an organization that desperately needed the best from its employees, step on those same employees in some kind of dysfunctional ritual dance. What is so interesting to me is that all the organizations for which I have worked (e.g., churches, a university, and a corporation) have experienced the same problems with the same results. Something fundamental is missing in the way people interact when they organize.

I was an organizational development consultant with a Fortune 500 energy company. The company had over 12,000 employees and had three platforms of business. Their oldest business was in regulated natural gas pipelines. They also had a group of non-regulated energy businesses that included everything from fuel refineries to convenience stores. The third business was the Energy, Marketing and Trading group. My role within the company was focused on team development, change management, and leadership development.

Disturbance

Language may be the greatest hurdle in the search for sustainable human systems. Which word should be the focal point of the discussion? Should it be *learning* or *change* or *transformation?* All describe what this book is about. For now, let's settle on *learning.*

Every learning process begins with some Disturbance—something that happens to an individual, either externally or internally, that begins his or her journey to greater awareness and new ways of thinking. I have come to realize that Disturbances come in all shapes and sizes. Some roll into our lives with the force of a hurricane, whereas others are mere whispers that we will surely miss if we are not paying close attention. Disturbances are sometimes welcomed, for they provide a new adventure. Other times, they invade on their own accord, forcing us to adapt to their whims. Regardless of their form, Disturbances are a natural part of the rhythm of life. By learning to pay attention to them, we can live more intentionally as the authors of our own journeys.

External Disturbance

What has been most interesting to me is that when I am open and listening closely to me and my life, many things become Disturbances. For instance, a movie can simply be entertainment or it can be the first step to new learning.

June 27, 1999

I am finding my way through the eyes of movie directors. It seems that right now, what opens my heart and my mind are the stories told in the movies I watch. At First Sight *is a movie about a man blind for life who gets a chance to see. The lesson learned for me came through the character Amy. She was his girlfriend who arranged for his medical miracle. In the end, she faced her fear. She let go of having to change people. She began for a moment to simply appreciate who a person is. I am convicted. Even though I am working on a way to explain to people how to free themselves, I am at the same time locking them in another prison. I am taking the process of overcoming fear and using it to validate myself. I know that I will fail both as a leader, a person, a father, and a husband unless I can truly let go and appreciate people for who they are. I don't know how to do this. I do not even know how to talk about it. I know that my message may be liberation, but I can never truly help people to be free unless I can let them be without changing them.*

I do not want to be misleading and give the impression that Disturbances are always curious events that stimulate comfortable learning cycles. Too often, Disturbances are frightening and painful. There is, quite often, no clear path ahead. I have had two such occurrences in the last several years: the health of my son, born October 5, 1999, and the death of a very close friend on November 28, 2000. The following excerpts reflect the intensity of this frightening, painful type of Disturbance.

October 24, 1999

In the last week, we have had some tests run on our son, Kobe. He seems healthy, but his breathing is too rapid. We do not know anything at this point, but one of the tests that they are running is sometimes associated with very difficult things like autism or retardation. It has been a bit nerve racking. On my way home from work on Friday, I began to think about the possibility of having a handicapped child and what that would mean. It is a great fear of mine. I guess because it would mean that I would never have any true independence again. As I thought about that, I became very much at ease. The thought that came to mind was that first it is life, Kobe being alive, that is the gift. There is no one kind of life that is right. I think this opened in me for the first time the experience that whatever he is, is an incredible gift that will enrich who I am. If growth is what I desire, I cannot grow independently. I can only grow in a relationship. The relationship with Kobe will open a part of me that could never have been reached before. I do not have words at this time to describe what I am trying to say.

February 11, 2001

I was unprepared as I opened the envelope. It still seems strange to look at Steve's name written on this death certificate. I read every detail and I felt a heavy sadness that is still untouched deep within me. This experience has been such a mixture of paradoxes. I experienced the greatest closeness to my friend in his last breath. Only the births of my children rival the profundity of this experience. His passing is both a tremendous loss and a marvelous opportunity. He has given me his company, Challenge Quest. I feel both a sense of responsibility and a great fear. Can I honor that gift by making the company successful? How will I make the transition from a relatively secure position with a large company to the unproven life of self-employment? Still at the edges of my mind, I wonder if this is my calling in life. How do you know which path to take when you cannot see beyond the hill right in front of you?

Like the hero in Joseph Campbell's mythic *The Hero's Journey*, we sometimes choose those things that will disturb us.[1] Other times, we stumble or fall into situations that set our lives in new directions. Not every Disturbance is of equal value, and not every one is worthy of our attention. One thing is for sure, however: we will continue to face Disturbances, and no amount of avoidance or denial will put an end to them.

Chaos

As you can tell from the journal entries so far, the phases of the model seem to collapse into one in real life. There is rarely any chronological break between Disturbance and Chaos or Chaos and Letting Go or even into Learning. Nevertheless, clear emotions are experienced as we become more aware of what we really believe. For me, I often experience Chaos as self-doubt, uncertainty, and anger.

Perhaps the real danger in times of Chaos is the amount of self-doubt that usually accompanies this phase. Not knowing for sure what lies ahead would not be nearly so painful if a deep questioning of self did not also fall in close proximity. Disturbance disrupts the balance that we think we have found. Once we are shaken awake, it is quite easy to question if we really know or are certain of anything at all.

June 20, 1999

I realize today that I feel absolutely helpless. The fact is that I have always wanted to enter a place, whether it is a class, a church, a university or a corporation, and help make it a better place. What I now know is that I have not done any of that. All of my fancy theories and plans, no matter how good they may be, are just other attempts to assume control. One person cannot change the system. I think I always fail because I want those places to change. That is the one thing they are all equipped not to do. I do not know how to help. My problem is that my dreams are always bigger than my station. I am not to be important—not in the way humans refer to. I am important because I live, but that, too, seems hollow at the moment. How do you participate in a system that is not very healthy and help it to be so without taking charge or being swallowed by the system in the process? If I cannot change the larger system, how can I change myself? And how should I change? Relationship and self-control are required to be a facilitating presence. Each day loses both of these. My patience is lacking. As I dare to become more involved, I realize how insignificant I am. This causes me to withdraw. As a result, I lose my connection/relationship with the system. I also lose any hope of helping. Maybe I am not to be a helper. If not, I do not know what I am to be. I do know that I am reading about too many people glamorizing business success and seeing market value as the ultimate measure of success. That is just not true. Help?

Uncertainty can have two faces. First, there is real confusion regarding the future, my purpose, and what direction I should take. Inwardly, it feels like life is very fragmented.

February 12, 2000

I have been restless of late. I am continually dissatisfied with my job, even though things internally seem to be changing for the better and we got a bonus. I believe it may be due to the fact that I am trying to satisfy my desire to make the world a better place and nurture my spirituality in my work. Corporate America is not conducive to such endeavors, except in small, out-of-the way places. I must return to nurturing my soul elsewhere. This will be a struggle, since I feel pressured by the amount of work I need to do to finish my doctoral studies and the dissonance I experience at church. Nonetheless, I, my work, and those around me will suffer if I do not shift my focus. I am unable to synthesize all this into one clear mindset. I must remain satisfied with a bit of fragmentation as I work through this.

The second face of uncertainty is an invigorating one. Standing at the edge of a brand-new adventure or challenge, we are also uncertain of the future. Yet that is part of the rush that brings us back to that edge over and over. I often experienced that vigor when I played basketball. Regardless of whether it was a sanctioned competitive game or a pick-up game at lunch, being able to take the last shot of the game was always a rush. The moment the ball left my hand, I knew I could be hero or scapegoat. I also knew that each time was another opportunity to do something I had never done before: win that particular game.

I am not sure if uncertainty, in and of itself, is good or bad. It has the characteristics of a polarity. The upside is that it generates anticipation and the energy to attempt something new. The downside of uncertainty is that it can be experienced as purposelessness and confusion. I do know that always demanding certainty is a 'Catch 22': We demand certainty because we fear uncertainty, yet that same fear will never really let us accept the certainty we may have. When it comes to uncertainty, we always have a choice: We can give power to our fear, or we can give voice to our hope. (Polarities will be discussed further in Chapter 6)

A third way I often experience Chaos is as anger. Uncertainty and self-doubt can generate powerful emotion. That emotion can leave us unbalanced and grasping for something to provide stability and direction. On occasion, that direction is to project that emotion outward in anger toward others.

September 18, 1999

It was a most unexpected reaction. Last Sunday, I went to church totally unaware of the violence that would be my response to the sermon. The pastor talked of gossip. He talked of the danger of gossip and the service to evil that it enrolls us in. He talked of the end that would come of such activity. In his haste to end such destructive work, he took what I thought was a shortcut. He played the "damnation by God" trump card on all who might not be convinced of his warning. I have been working for some time at listening within in order to let go and learn. This day, I was caught totally unaware. My anger and vengeance that were focused at the pastor were extreme. He had punched all the right buttons, and I had not prepared myself to consider alternative ways of taking it all in. I returned to him the very judgment he had dished out. This was an eye-opener for me. I must continue to consider what this means. I am enraged at attempts to bully and dominate others, even if it is for their own good. I desire authenticity and consistency in leaders. I cannot forget that they are only human, too. I do not know what I should do, but I must stay connected to this situation in order to respond in a way different than in the past. Getting angry, venting to others, and running away is no longer sufficient. How do I express myself without diminishing those I am addressing? How can I truly live the Gospel that I say I believe?

I should note that the anger is not the Chaos. It is merely a sign as to the intensity of the Chaos. It can be made worse by denying that it exists. Pretending that we do not feel what we feel only fuels the anger. I have come to realize that I must be cautious as to how I express the anger. However, if I want to move beyond it, I must begin with acknowledging its presence.

Letting Go

How can we tell if we are Letting Go and thus moving toward learning? When we let go of our need for certainty, comfort, and control, we are making the transition to Learning. Yet how can you know if you are really letting these things go or just doing what you are supposed to do? When our actions move us toward taking personal responsibility, rather than being victims, we are at the threshold of Letting Go.

Another way of thinking about personal responsibility is to consider how we contribute to the situation at hand. It is always easier to recognize the shortcomings of others. When we begin to Let Go, we become aware of our own contributions to what is happening. Rather than blame others, we take responsibility for what is ours—no more and no less.

December 23, 2000

It is only today that I am really clear about the internal disturbance that has emerged from my departure from the university position that I held. It would be easy to let the injustice and corruption of a university administrator fuel my anger. But now I see. Learning and Disturbance merge into a new beginning as I realize what the real message is. Whatever I experience in this fragmented world, I play a part. I contribute in some way to furthering institutions that resemble this one. It would be easy to place blame, but to do so would be to perpetuate the hollowness that I resent.

The awareness that began that day and the many days after has begun to grow clearer. I am not playing a martyr in this story. I did not deserve to be treated as I was. I was not, however, without responsibility. I lived within this community and perpetuated its ways. What ways am I talking about? The ways included allowing my own insecurity to create distance between others and myself. I lived at more than an arm's distance away. The cause of my dismissal was a lack of trust. They could not trust me because they did not truly know me. They listened to what I said, but they never knew the life behind the words. In this way, I contributed to a system based on politeness, formality, and an outward image. I was too busy furthering the "cause" and running from my own fear to take the time to listen to their concerns. Again, I believe those responsible for my dismissal were driven by their own insecurities and egos. They fought their own demons and used their positions of leadership to benefit themselves, to reinforce their illusions of security, certainty, and validation. But unless I can seek a different way, I will be just like them.

Learning

The result of Letting Go is being more open to new ideas, new ways of interacting, and new perspectives. In particular, I am willing to influence and to be influenced. At the same time, Learning leads us into the next Disturbance. With a newfound calm, I can dare to ask more difficult questions that I could not consider when I was afraid.

So now, I face a new challenge. If leadership essentially provides the potential for good or evil, how can I be a leader without doing harm? Another imperative question is: What does the current circumstance require of a leader?

I have come to believe that the answers to both questions come in my response to the forces surrounding change. How I respond to ambiguity, complexity, diversity, and power will determine the type of influence I will have. In addition, my ability to understand and determine my own responses to such forces, rather than the responses of others, is what will ultimately enable those around me to live in a healthier manner.

Synthesis thinking is a better response to ambiguity. Ambiguity requires critical thinking and exploration, since its essence is unclear. The ability to think in terms of both/and, rather than either/or, opens the creative possibility that ambiguity offers. How is this important to leadership? Synthesis thinking is the foundation to solidarity. I came to realize that much of my fearfulness was a result of only focusing on the differences between others and me. I could not see my experience mirrored in the lives of others. I could only hear the differences. I could not comprehend the similarity of the questions that others and I were asking. Consequently, I could not appreciate the truth that a perspective other than my own could contribute to my understanding. I could only perceive difference as possible confrontation and rejection. The way I thought left me fragmented from a community that I desperately wanted to be a part of.

I have since learned to listen deeply to the conversations of others. Their unique perspectives assist me in clarifying my own thinking. As a result, ambiguity is not something threatening but rather an opportunity to learn, grow, and mature. What I have come to realize is that not fearing ambiguity allows me to create an atmosphere for others to not be afraid, either. I now know that leadership is to serve others by helping them ask the important but frightening questions that we all must ask if we are to discover meaning and purpose.

The twin sister of ambiguity is complexity. Where either/or thinking seeks certainty in ambiguity, the fearful seek simplicity in complexity. Again, the danger is maintaining a myopic view of the world. A fearful response to complexity does not appreciate the mystery of life. A tremendous void of meaning has trapped us all into the pursuit of quick-fix solutions. Leading others has been reduced to giving clear instructions and making sure everyone follows those instructions explicitly.

Such was the type of leadership that I did not want to follow or embody. But what other possible response to complexity is there? My belief is that only when we can embrace the need for transcendent meaning can we lead in a manner that creates freedom for others, rather than fear. The critical questions I have asked are: What makes me valuable? Why am I important? My thought is now that value and importance must be accepted by faith. Value and importance are gifts from a Creator that has fashioned us all in the creative forces of love and acceptance. For much of my life, I lived in such a way as to prove my value. But the more I tried, the less I believed I was making progress. If utility was what defined me, then I could not admit when I failed. Failure was a manifestation of not being useful. Being wrong, then, was an affront to my identity.

> *If leadership essentially provides the potential for good or evil, how can I be a leader without doing harm?*

I came to the conclusion some time ago that utility is not what defines me. The implication for leadership is that the role of the leader is not to ensure that those who follow him or her are never wrong; instead, truly fulfilling the leader's role means helping others learn from their own experience. Before people can learn from their experience, they must be grounded in their own individual sense of value. Only then will they have the courage to ask better questions. Only in asking better questions can sustainable solutions be found to complex situations.

Diversity is a third driving force of change. Much has been written in the last ten years about the need for leaders to bring others together. I recently was sent a picture from the front page of the Wall Street Journal showing a professional holding a sign on the sidewalk that read, "Collaborate or die." The fundamental issue in fostering collaboration is difference.

I remember talking with a young facilitator with whom I had worked. As we talked about how the group had gone that day, he spoke of his frustration. "I get frustrated working with groups who just don't get it." I saw him live this out. The more the group "did not get it," the more he tried to force them to.

My response to him was to ask, "I wonder what would happen if you could focus more on what they were getting rather than what they were not?"

We will never lead well until we can accept that leadership is not primarily about getting others to do what we want them to do. If we require from others what they cannot or will not give us, we create an environment that is violent. In this sense, difference is not a gift but a problem to solve. Leadership is about appreciating the uniqueness of the other. In that appreciation, we can come to understand why they do what they do. Curiosity fosters inclusivity. Inclusivity embodies all the strength of difference.

Unfortunately, we are not capable of always accepting difference. At times, our uniqueness is used for self-interest. Fear causes us to do things to each other that are hurtful. Consequently, inclusivity is only possible among people who know how to forgive. Forgiveness requires us to let go of things that keep us alienated and fragmented. When we forgive one another, we must let go of the need to be justified, the need to be validated, and the need to be right. I have only recently realized that the power of forgiveness is not to change the other; rather, it is a response that changes me. Too much that occurs in the name of forgiveness has little to do with restoring relationships. Relationships are healthy when there is mutual influence. For me, forgiveness is too often simply an agreement not to seek retribution. This is not forgiveness. Such an agreement has not restored the equality necessary for mutual influence. The mishap of the other has been used to gather power over him or her.

Power and the use of power is the final test for true leadership. True leaders create power by giving it away. Forgiveness is an example. If I change my view of the other person and give away my need to be right, justified, and validated, I free them to respond differently to me. By changing me, I provide freedom for those around me to choose a new and better way.

Conclusion

If I were to return to my newfound paradox of leadership, it would lead me to recognize that leading is not only about giving power away. Many times, much damage is done because leaders do nothing. Power unused is just as destructive as power misused. The critical need is to learn to be a steward of power. Sometimes, the greatest gift of a leader is to set boundaries. In this sense, power can be wielded to create greater security for others. At other times, the potential in others can be unleashed by not using your own knowledge, skill and position.

Theory

The next two chapters broaden the conversation once again. Understanding the dynamics or the decision points in the differentiation process does not in and of itself lead to differentiation. There are four core learning abilities that enable the insight and character to begin to define self. The next chapter presents these core abilities.

Once a leader begins to develop their level of differentiation, the next great question is how can he or she help others develop their capacity for self-differentiation? How can a leader influence others without limiting their future capability to be mature and take personal responsibility for their actions? Unless a critical mass of any team or organization pursues self-differentiation, there is little likelihood of sustainability. Yet with the right attention, leaders can continue to create the conditions that bring individuals to the critical crossroads of self definition.

Chapter 5 - The Four Core Learning Abilities

*"Courage is not the absence of fear;
It is the belief that there is something
more important than our fear."*
Ambrose Redmoon

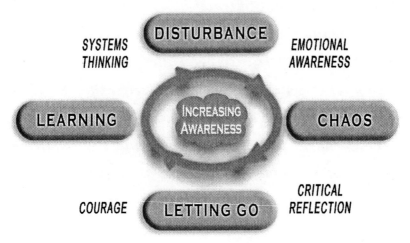

FIGURE 5.1

There are four core learning abilities that individually are necessary but not sufficient on their own for leaders to develop: Emotional Awareness, Critical Reflection, Courage, and Systems Thinking. These abilities are skills that are used in furthering the learning dynamic described in chapter three.

But more than that, these abilities orient your thinking in such a way that you will more likely notice the learning dynamic in the first place. Furthermore, as your abilities grow, it becomes possible to participate in the learning dynamic rather than inhibit it.

Emotional Awareness

It is no accident that Emotional Awareness is the first core learning ability to be addressed. The path from Disturbance to the more fully developed awareness of Chaos tends primarily to be an emotional journey. Chaos is usually experienced as an emotion first and as thinking second. Learning to pay attention to what is happening within is the first benefit of Emotional Awareness.

Emotional Awareness is the ability to listen inward. Although emotional process (our natural ability to take in information from the environment and respond to it) is more than feelings, a beginning point to understanding the emotional process is to begin listening to your feelings. There is a foundational truth that underlies this point. Human activity is an ongoing process made up of three mutually influencing forces: emotions, thinking, and behavior. Embedded in all behavior are assumptions. The difficulty is that assumptions are mostly automated within the human mind and, consequently, difficult to reach directly. What is needed is a passage that will indirectly lead to uncovering assumptions. Behavior and emotions provide that passage. Behavior is observable not only by the one acting but by others, as well. As such, it provides a tangible place of beginning as you seek to uncover assumptions. Emotions provide a similar departure point. It has been said that sound decisions are not made with emotion. Emotions can be fickle, irrational, and unfounded. Yet despite all that, emotions always tell us what we believe at that moment. Strong emotion is a signal that something important is happening. Rather than seek relief from the tyranny of anger, frustration, fear, or reluctance, if these emotions can be explored, they will provide a window to the soul, which can lead to substantial understanding.

Emotional Awareness does not simply stop with becoming more articulate about your feelings. A deeper understanding is to be had here. Emotional Awareness is an attempt to understand the system as a whole. When people come together to form some kind of lasting relationship, they create an emotional field.[1] Even short lived contact can create such a field. Consider mob behavior during riots. This recognition takes Emotional Awareness beyond individual feelings to consider the systemic nature of the emotional process.[2]

Emotional process "enables an organism to receive information (from within itself and its environment), to integrate that information and to respond on the basis of it".[3] All living organisms have this type of response as a matter of survival. Unless people are intentional about choosing the type of response to a situation, the automatic response will be some form of "fight or flight." Each person comes into any relationship with his or her own definition and experiences of threat—that is, those things that raise his or her level of anxiety. When groups form, families come together, or companies incorporate, shared perceptions of threat come into being. That threat may take the form of the amount of directness experienced in face-to-face interaction, or it may be the unspoken rules associated with the formal and informal power structures in an organization. Whatever the form of the threat, once the system has been established, individuals will perceive something as threatening that in a different set of relationships would not be seen in this light.

> **When individuals take personal responsibility to become intentional about how they respond to the world around them, the collective perception of threat can be changed.**

Emotional Awareness, when combined with the other three learning abilities, allows for a type of Learning that shifts the emotional field. In other words, when individuals take personal responsibility to become intentional about how they respond to the world around them, the collective perception of threat can be changed. For instance, in teams in which learning is truly valued, to speak of failure is no longer perceived as dangerous. The mental model for what is acceptable to speak of collectively has been changed. It is only possible to achieve this kind of Learning when you are aware of the emotional process of the field created by the relationship.

Here is another example of the dynamics of emotional fields. Everyone has trigger points—those subjects, tones, expressions, or attitudes that initiate powerful responses within us. Often, the origin of the trigger point is not even consciously remembered. Isaacs speaks of listening from Disturbance:

> *Often when we listen to others we may discover that we are listening from disturbance; in other words, we are listening from an emotional memory rather than from the present moment. If I say something to you that you do not like, you may be triggered by what I say, perhaps intensely so. Your future listening will be colored for a while by this.*[4]

The truth is we all carry a multitude of emotional memories that continue to affect us years after the events that formed the memories occurred. The effect of this emotional field—the forces brought into existence through participation in our families, work groups, schools, and friendships—transcends time, unless we become aware and intentional about the responses we make. It will be nearly impossible to uncover our emotional triggers and their associated assumptions without the assistance of the responses of others.

This line of thinking requires attention to two other terms critical to understanding emotional process: anxiety and reactivity. *Anxiety* is the emotional response to a perceived threat. Understanding anxiety's impact on the system is a primary key to learning that results in being aware, intentional, and coherent. Anxiety results from any number of situations. Ambiguity, complexity, time pressure, fear of uncertainty, lack of control, possibility of failure, and embarrassment will signal those learned actions that will relieve anxiety for the individual.

The impact of anxiety on the system is that it creates automatic, reflexive responses, or *reactivity*. The particular form of ones reactivity is learned from experience. But regardless of the particular form of a reactive response, like was discussed in Chapter three, it is usually the least creative, least effective response to the situation. An example of this is when I took a class from a particular professor that was a colleague of mine. He taught a general education course on health and physical fitness. He took his subject quite seriously. I on the other hand, believed I could pass the physical requirements so I spent our class time exploring a local creek rather than following his training regiment. He caught me one day. This left me feeling uncomfortable when I was around him. Part of it was his demeanor, but a great deal of it was my own embarrassment for having behaved rather childishly in his class. The amount of grief I eventually experienced by not taking care of the past, and thereby winning him as an ally, far outweighed any momentary anxiety that would have resulted from having to be honest with him. My reactive response was to avoid this professor. The more I avoided the professor the higher the level of mistrust, or at least misunderstanding, grew between us. Eventually it was just one more item that made me look bad and kept me outside the accepted social system of the university. I should have accepted my discomfort and tried to build a bridge to him.

Resistance to change often has a reactive nature. Resistance is an emotional response to change that signals something important is at hand. Sometimes, resistance is a legitimate response to an invasive action that threatens appropriate boundaries. On the other hand, resistance can also be a reactive response to a lack of self-awareness. It works like this: Someone presents a new idea or a proposed change, and the immediate response is to back away. What makes this reactive is that it is not the merit of the idea that is rejected but rather the nature of the idea—namely, that it is different from what is being done in the present. If you do not know what to think on the matter, you will take a defensive stance.

Emotional Awareness can reveal the inner processes at work, particularly those reactive responses to anxiety-provoking situations. It also opens your perception to include the system dynamics that often cause the deep-seated, chronic difficulties experienced in relationships.

Critical Reflection

The second core learning ability is Critical Reflection. Like the other core learning abilities, it is a skill, an intention, and a mindset. Critical Reflection is the underlying methodology through which the other abilities operate. As a skill, Critical Reflection is the ability to ask important questions—questions that unsettle the dust and allow our assumptions, which have remained just out of consciousness, to step into the light. Critical Reflection seeks to uncover the underlying assumptions that form the basis of how you see the world. As an intention, Critical Reflection seeks to make meaning from experience. A critical role for leaders is to help others make sense of the world they are experiencing. That is possible only if you can make meaning of your own experience. As a mindset, Critical Reflection reminds people that they must slow down to speed up. Critical Reflection recognizes that a balance must be struck between action and reflection. Real learning requires inner work. Perhaps the most important work of leadership is seeking an inner clarity and self-awareness.

> **Resistance is an emotional response to change that signals something important is at hand.**

"Which questions guide our lives? Which questions do we make our own? Which questions deserve our undivided attention and full personal commitment? Finding the right questions is as crucial as finding the right answers."[5] Self-defined leadership is predicated on Critical Reflection—asking important questions. These are questions that look beyond the obvious to see what else is going on. Instead of just asking "How can I feel better?" this type of thinking goes a step beyond and asks "What is it about this experience that elicits this emotion within me?" Instead of looking for simple cause-and-effect answers, Critical Reflection probes deeper in order to see the multiple variables that create any situation. Exploring why you feel or act in certain ways will allow you to use behavior and emotion as a doorway into a deeper understanding of your thinking. The individual who does not ask such questions will continue on a mistaken pathway long after experience has told him or her to assume a new direction. This skill of questioning will enable the intention and the mindset of Critical Reflection to be accomplished.

"Leaders learn most often from their experiences—especially their failures. Too often, though, they miss the lessons. They lack the reflective capacity to learn on their own."[6] The intention of Critical Reflection is to continue learning in order that self-differentiation may result. If this is to happen, you must learn to pay attention to and reflect on your experiences. Unfortunately, leaders do not typically practice the type of reflection that draws out the lessons of the experiences of life nor do they typically pass on that ability to those who follow them. Asking critical questions that seek to uncover the lessons of experience will enable a group to make use of the great potential of collective learning. Critically reflecting on experience is essential to uncover the assumptions that underlie chosen behavior. Every experience is an opportunity for learning. It is either an opportunity to see the world more clearly or to continue to suffer the influence of illusions and unchallenged assumptions.

Asking questions does require a shift in mindset. Reflection is a practice that takes time and space. It cannot happen in a panic. It is countercultural to most organizations. The mindset of Critical Reflection recognizes an underlying continuum of learning; there must be a balance of both action and reflection, of doing and being. Over time, both ends of the continuum are necessary for health. The Industrial Revolution, with its accelerating technological advances, has magnified action to the exclusion of reflection. The result has been a diminished capacity to think critically, to uncover ineffective patterns of behavior, and to take responsibility for your own life.

A result of pausing to think critically about your reactions and experiences—and thus to uncover the assumptions that frame the world—is the ability to see things as they really are. For leaders, those who would intentionally seek to influence the systems of which they are a part, the "acid test is their ability to preserve their own hold on reality, to see things as they really are, in spite of the pressures from people around them".[7] It is no easy matter to form a clear picture of what is really going on. There are too many who would collude to have leaders see what they want, rather than what is. That is, to some extent, a characteristic of us all. It is particularly the case when there are high levels of anxiety and reactivity. Individuals who are not aware of themselves have difficulty separating what actually is from what they feel. Their perception is their reality. The result of not seeing reality is that leaders cast their own shadows on those who surround them. As described by Palmer:

> *A leader is someone with the power to project either shadow or light onto some part of the world and onto the lives of the people who dwell there. . . . But by failing to look at our shadows, we feed a dangerous delusion that leaders too often indulge: that our efforts are always well intended, our power is always benign, and the problem is always in those difficult people whom we are trying to lead.*[8]

Thus, the practice of Critical Reflection leads people headlong into the ability of Courage, for without taking a long look into what each individual really is, Critical Reflection will be an elementary practice of idle speculation.

Courage

Courage is not an easy concept to define. It is even harder to develop because it is an attitude, rather than a skill set or technique. Nevertheless, in the context of perpetuating deep learning in both yourself and others, Courage will be described in the context of emotional stamina, an appreciation of mystery, and the ability to acknowledge limitation.

Emotional stamina is a critical concept in the process of differentiation. It is the ability to be comfortable enough with discomfort long enough to be intentional with your choices. It is this ability to go first and stay the course that indicates the maturity of leadership. As mentioned earlier, it is the experience of discomfort that sends many people into automatic reactions to situations in order to feel better. In the context of self-defined leadership, Courage is the ability to face the reality of yourself and to manage your fear in order to operate from a position of freedom rather than fear.

Starting with your own fear is the first step in this learning process. Unless you are willing to touch your own pain and insecurity, you will not be able to assist others through theirs. And it is only when the individual can wade through some discomfort that real learning and sustainable change occur. Too many of the actions of leaders, though perceived as attempts to be helpful, are really automatic reactions to the discomfort of others. Many who assert themselves in the service of others are really trying to move those others along so that they, the helpers, will not be uncomfortable. "One of the hardest things we must do sometimes is to be present to another person's pain without trying to 'fix' it, to simply stand respectfully at the edge of that person's mystery and misery."[9]

The practice of such Courage will be experienced as powerlessness. A reactive strategy is to give advice. Palmer notes that this will not work toward the greater freedom of the person that needs the help. "In an effort to avoid those feelings, I give advice, which sets me, not you, free."[10] An example of this can be seen on a challenge/ropes course. A challenge course often uses events that require people to climb high into the air—namely, a thirty-five-foot climbing wall. When a climber appears stuck, the first reaction of those on the ground is to yell directions. Outwardly, this seems only a helpful gesture. However, seeing it through the eyes of the system, those shouts of direction may be an attempt to make those on the ground feel less tense. If the person climbing can move on, then those on the ground do not have to endure the discomfort of seeing a team member struggle.

If anything can be learned from the concept of emotional stamina it is that a leader's greatest test is to be able to stand alone. This component is often neglected in the pursuit of leadership. As a result, leaders often sacrifice character in order to gain acceptance and avoid the pain of being alone. On the other hand, Friedman suggests at least five ways a leader will sometimes stand alone: (1) stepping outside the emotional climate of the day in order to see possibilities that others cannot see, (2) being willing to be exposed as one takes stands, (3) standing firm in the face of resistance and downright rejection, (4) remaining true to self in the face of sabotage, and (5) relentlessly pursuing their vision.[11] Friedman says these were the characteristics of the great explorers that freed Europe from the Dark Ages. In their totality, these traits at least shine a light on the darkness that differentiated leaders must endure. Let's look at these five points of loneliness that leaders must face.

Stepping outside the emotional climate of the day is not an easy task. And even if you are able to accomplish this feat, the result may include a nagging sense of just being crazy. Stepping outside the anxiety and reactivity of the moment takes a leap of faith. For example, in the movie *The American President,* Michael Douglas's character, the president, finds himself in a heated political stewpot in an election year.[12] His antagonist, a senator played by Richard Dreyfus, pulls no punches in this political brawl. What is interesting about this story is that the senator understands the power of anxiety for winning elections. He attacks the sitting president on a number of fronts. Initially, the president does nothing, hoping not to get caught in the escalating emotion the senator is creating. However, this non-response is one of two expected responses to the situation, a counterattack being the other. If the president acts either with a withdrawal or a counterattack, he is playing into the regressed political system of the day. I say regressed because it is a system with limited imagination, high levels of reactivity, and low levels of personal responsibility.

It is not until the president's final press conference, held just before the State of the Union address, that we see true leadership. With all his aides caught up in the same reactive system, berating him with advice about counterattacks, he steps outside that climate of 'protect ones position at all costs' and sees another way. The answer he gives is less important at this point. What is important is that for him as a leader, there was a third possible response. However, it was a response that could not have been seen in the swirling chaos of the reactive emotion at hand. The president had to get beyond the prevailing emotional process of the system in order to free his imagination. That action would inevitably result in a creative response. The third possibility was to stand up and take appropriate personal responsibility, to say out loud what was really going on, and to clearly state his own vision of the future. Not getting caught up in the reactivity of others is essential to leadership.

In fact, the moment a leader steps outside that emotional process and before others see their way clear to join a new path, he or she is out there all alone. This stepping out to imagine a new way leaves a leader terribly exposed. Leaders who cannot or will not suffer the "dis-ease" of standing alone will always adapt to the least mature member of the system.[13] As a result, the organization will suffer at the hand of the leader's own fear of being alone. Fearing a loss of comfort, a leader often seeks to adapt to those who make the most noise. Consequently, the organization is held captive to the desires of those least able to see anything beyond their own need.

> *Emotional Stamina is the ability to be comfortable enough with discomfort long enough to be intentional with your choices.*

The third way leaders will sometimes have to stand alone is being able to face resistance and rejection. Any movement of change will unleash some form of resistance in the system. This resistance derives from the natural desire to keep things the same. If you act in Courage, you must "overcome the voice inside that constantly gnaws at you, asking 'How can you have it right and everyone else be crazy?'"[14] Helping others move toward a broader perspective requires the capacity first to consider what most do not see as possible. Otherwise, the way would be more obvious. To be able to practice this requires a mindset that can make clear bold observations yet not have your own personal sense of value dependent on other people acting or even accepting the observations.

Paradoxically, the Courage to not need people to change in accordance with your own perspective is exactly what will allow others to take a potentially threatening observation and not run from it. Resistance is to be expected. It is a natural consequence of important things happening. Resistance does not need to hold you captive. Fear of change does not have to be paralyzing. It can be an opportunity to discover something new. Leaders who help others learn are prepared to experience resistance and not run from it or deny it.

Sabotage is a more active form of resistance that leaders will need to be conscious of and the fourth way they will sometimes stand alone. Unlike a simple act of hesitancy or disagreement, sabotage is an action designed to return the differentiating leader to their role in the system. As Friedman describes it, sabotage can be an undercutting of a leader or seduction[15]. Undercutting is easier to see. This occurs when someone uses political influence, position and power, or simply making a leader look bad in order to control him. There is a terrific example of this in the movie *Instinct*.[16] In the story, a psychiatrist(Cuba Gooding, Jr) is attempting to do a once-in-a-lifetime analysis of a very famous scientist(Anthony Hopkins) who lived several years with apes. In addition, the psychiatrist is required to provide services to the mentally ill individuals in the prison where the scientist is being held. The law requires that each person be allowed to go outside on a regular basis. The guards have instituted a practice whereby only the inmate who draws the ace of diamonds from a deck of cards gets to go outside. But the effect of this practice is that the biggest inmate takes the card away from whoever happens to get it each day. This works for the guards because it keeps the inmates focused on someone else other than the guards.

The psychiatrist in the movie, believing this is unjust, takes responsibility to change the system. Rather than draw cards, each inmate's name is placed in a box and whomever's name is drawn that day will go outside. This will continue until everyone has a turn. This, of course, greatly disrupts the system. The dominant inmate is upset because he is no longer allowed to act without consideration of others. The guards are upset because it undermines their system of control. At one point, in the scene when the confrontation is coming to a head, the prison gym is in total chaos. The psychiatrist, though, understands the greater good, which lies beyond squelching the chaos. By holding their ground, the inmates, though mentally limited, stand up and take responsibility for their own decisions about choosing who will go outside. By not placing his own comfort ahead of progress, the psychiatrist raises the level of personal responsibility in the whole group.

Just after this scene, the warden meets him in the break room. There was no discussion of why Cuba's character did what he did or the benefits to the prisoners. The warden simply used his position of power to threaten Cuba's character from having access to Anthony Hopkins' character. This was an obvious undercutting form of sabotage to get Cuba's character back in line. With seduction, members of a group or organization will play on a leader's compassion or friendship to get the leader to back off their vision and differentiated responses and return to the status quo. Either way, the leader must be willing to be alone if he/she is able to not be taken in by sabotage.

The larger point to be made about Courage is that leaders must maintain the pursuit of their vision which is the fifth way leaders will stand alone. This enables them to pursue necessary courses of action when others would waffle for fear of discontent. It is not that well-differentiated leaders do not experience discontent as uncomfortable; rather, mature leaders understand that, at some point, it is imperative to stand firm, even if this means standing alone. Courage is the ability to choose progress over peace. Those who are less mature will see this as being bullheaded, selfish, or mean. Those who would aspire to what is possible will recognize this strength and draw on it to pursue their own learning and change. An example of this might be how transparent leaders allow themselves to be in front of their people. I was once called in to facilitate a planning retreat for a vice president of human relations and her direct reports. This group was made up with very seasoned and intelligent people. However, they continued to be limited by dependency upon the leader and mistrust with one another. During the session it became obvious as to why there was so much dependency on the leader. A team member would ask a question and the V.P. would give a five minute monologue as to what should be done. I mentioned to her that those kind of responses would tend to make her reports less sure of acting on their own. In front of the group she asked for some coaching. She asked me how she might behave differently to get a different result. For the rest of the day, she was intent on asking better questions and helping the group discover their own answers. It was her courage to ask for help and then intentionally practice what she had been told that allowed the rest of the members to begin to take responsibility for their own actions. Ultimately, if Learning is to occur, the leader's vision of what is true and healthy must be pursued relentlessly, even if it disrupts the system.

> *The Courage to not need people to change in accordance with your own perspective is exactly what will allow others to take a potentially threatening observation and not run from it.*

In addition to Emotional Stamina that raises your threshold for tolerating discomfort, a courageous leader has a deep *appreciation for mystery*:

> *Mystery surrounds every deep experience of the human heart: the deeper we go into the heart's darkness or its light, the closer we get to the ultimate*

mystery of God. But our culture wants to turn mysteries into puzzles to be explained or problems to be solved, because maintaining the illusion that we can "straighten things out" makes us feel powerful. Yet mysteries never yield to solutions or fixes—and when we pretend that they do, life becomes not only more banal but also more hopeless, because the fixes never work.[17]

For most of the last four hundred years, the Western culture has been running at top speed away from the inherent mystery of the universe. People fear what they cannot explain and thus control. Consequently, they can never experience true sustainable change, because deep learning requires, if but for a moment, letting go of what is known and reaching out for what might be. This is a matter of faith, not reason. Courage does not require certainty. It leaves room for the unexplainable.

Mystery is the point at which Courage connects back with *transcendent meaning.* How is this relevant to Learning? To begin, it promotes a faith that more is happening than can be seen. What you can sense is not the final word on your being or possibility. There are things that are real beyond those things which can be confirmed with your senses. This is crucial to creating space for Learning. This has not been the paradigm of the modern mindset or the scientific revolution. Running from an age of oppressive spiritual institutions and the ignorance of superstition, science offered the possibility that everything could be explained and thus controlled. It has been the rise of the "new sciences" that has moved the rational community back toward an appreciation of mystery. Realizing that there is more going on than you can see leads to a watchfulness that can help you participate in what is occurring.

If this idea is extended a bit further, it can lead to an essential belief that provides the strength to let go. It is the belief that a person is more than his or her actions, both the successes and the failures. Each individual possesses an innate value. It is this sense of value that supports the courage not to react. Learning that is intent on greater awareness, intentionality, and coherence requires a willingness not to always be right. Moreover, it requires the ability to be wrong without being reactive. This is not possible if being right and not being wrong are central to what makes you valuable.

This belief not only affects your view of yourself, but it also defines how you see others. Seeing the innate value in the humanness of others allows you not to pressure them into being a certain way. It allows patience for others to find their own way, rather than the need for them to accept your way. It also provides the relaxed presence to be curious about the other's way so that you can be influenced by the other's perspective. It is the confident belief that an individual's value is a gift of creation that forms a strong sense of self. It is this sense of self that keeps systems—whether families, teams, or organizations—from being overwhelmed with the need for everyone to be the same.

The appreciation of mystery—the belief that more is going on than you can see—sets you free from the belief that if anything is going to be done, you must be the one to do it. This *ability to acknowledge limitation* is the third component of Courage. There is an incredible need for watchfulness in this process of learning and change. Such attention is not possible if you believe that all positive movement is a result of your busyness. There is more at work than can be seen, explained or controlled. "This discovery leads to a paradoxical integrity of surrender, surrendering into commitment. Sometimes the greatest acts of commitment involve doing nothing but sitting and waiting until I just know what to do next."[18] In the end, the most courageous acts may involve doing nothing intentionally.

Systems Thinking

Only rarely does a truly new paradigm emerge. Most breakthroughs are only new openings in familiar pathways. One fundamental shift that truly changed the pace and direction of thought in the twentieth century was *Systems Thinking*.[19] Systems Thinking, the fourth core learning ability, is an orientation to the world that seeks to view the elements in relation to the whole.

It is important to recognize that Systems Thinking is a foundational influence for the learning model in this book. Namely, the ideas of living or complex adaptive systems have provided the most guidance.[20] In this section, the following five ideas, which have been adapted from systems theory, are essential to understanding the learning dynamic and thus this model of leadership:

1. Healthy systems promote individuals who are capable of taking personal responsibility yet have an awareness of the whole.
2. In healthy systems, individuals recognize and respect boundaries.
3. Living systems are organized around identity.
4. Living systems have stability over time because they are constantly changing.
5. In order to understand systems, one needs to respect the principle of emergence.

If sustainable health is the desired outcome, it is essential to promote personal responsibility but with an awareness of what effect your actions may have on the larger system. Too much energy is wasted in organizations trying to get other people to change. If Learning is to occur that leads to greater awareness, intentionality, and coherence, attention must be placed on raising the level of personal responsibility while also understanding the influence that acting on that responsibility will have on the system. Rather than try to force others to change or to wait for a hero to arrive and force such change, a systemic leader seeks to understand his or her own contribution to the current state. Such understanding gives you real power to influence change. Living systems are in a state of constant mutual adaptation. Trying to force others to change increases the anxiety and thus reactivity in the system. This mutual adaptation will be away from Learning, moving toward greater distance and eventually greater immaturity in the system. However, taking charge of changing your own behavior in order to influence the system's processes promotes greater maturity and sets the stage for real Learning.

> *Courage does not require certainty. It leaves room for the unexplainable.*

Taking personal responsibility is only half of the equation. If you are unaware of the whole set of interdependent relationships of which you are a part, the personal responsibility that results will be very selfish. At best, your actions will result in a plethora of unintended consequences. At worst, there will be anarchy. In healthy organizations, members do not serve only themselves. That is, they serve themselves only to the extent that it promotes well-being in the larger system. Leaders who seek to influence the systems they are a part of will always try to understand themselves in the context of the systemic relationships. Such leaders will try to influence others by changing themselves first. Thus, learning and change in a living system is always a freely chosen pursuit.

The recognition of boundaries is the second critical component to Systems Thinking. This recognition grows out of and supports the first component. It is a focus on self-awareness and self-regulation that promotes the creation of sustainable systems.

In order to clarify the concept of boundaries, consider the immune system of the human body as a useful parallel. The fundamental action of the immune system is to discover that which is not part of the body and remove it. The protection of the body's integrity maintains health. The leader who truly pursues Learning that increases awareness, intentionality, and coherence will understand and respect the boundaries of others. The concept of boundaries results in two important corollaries: (1) Systems that understand boundaries organize toward strength rather than weakness and (2) A healthy understanding of boundaries creates a humility necessary for the survival of the whole.

There are two ways to maintain health: by completely removing all pathogens or by strengthening the immune system. The first path focuses on what is wrong or what might cause disease. This is an orientation toward weakness. The difficulty with this plan is that some level of pathogen is necessary to equip the system fully to withstand other invasions. Removing all the pathogens or threats does not promote Learning and strength; rather, it weakens the system's ability to do either. The other option is to focus on strengthening the immune system. This requires an intentional effort to gain more clarity about who you are and what it is that you believe. Self-awareness is a prerequisite for self-regulation.

> *Organizing toward your strengths indicates that it is more rewarding in the long run to encourage those who are changing than it is to try to convince those who would not change.*

This idea of organizing toward strength can be extended a bit further. It provides a sense of direction for leaders who seek to influence the system. This principle indicates that it is more rewarding in the long run to encourage those who are changing than it is to try to convince those who would not change. The consequence of not doing so is the herding dynamic of anxious systems. As was discussed in Friedman's second way leaders will face loneliness earlier in this chapter, the least mature, least adaptive individuals take all the energy and resources of the system so that those who do seek growth are stunted or ignored. To enact this principle of encouraging those who desire to change, the leader must start with himself or herself and find others who are open to influence.

Here is an example. I was asked by a manager to assess her team. The team atmosphere was full of tension and much of the frustration was being focused on the manager. At the center of this group's difficulties was a woman who was very insecure, inept and unmotivated to improve. She was fearful of taking responsibility even for things that she already knew how to do. The manager did not know what to do with this woman. Her first strategy was to ask the rest of the team to adapt to this woman. Consequently, the more mature team members spent enormous amounts of energy explaining things over and over or just avoiding the woman. This was a staff that was short handed and they were spending a large sum of money on an assistant that could not even file. As the team's frustration with this woman grew and it became clear that the manager was not going to act they turned their focus to the manager. My intervention began by working with the manager. She came to the realization that part of the reason the unproductive worker was not confronted was the manager's own anxiety about confrontation. I encouraged her to define boundaries around this woman and not to require the mature workers to conform to her. I also helped the manager prepare for the sabotage she was likely to experience from the unproductive worker. The second part of the intervention was to refocus the manager's energy towards empowering and rewarding the productive workers rather than trying to change the one which did not want to change. In a short period of time, the problem employee was gone and the group made some very real progress towards a more healthy and productive work atmosphere.

The third principle of Systems Thinking extends the previous two. It says that all living systems organize around identity. The consequence of such a principle is that if lasting change is to occur, it must focus on the level of identity.[21] If an individual is really to change, he or she must challenge the assumptions that form the foundation of how he or she sees and makes meaning of the world. To do so not only changes behavior but changes the internal logic of choices. Thus, Critical Reflection is an activity of healthy systems. Reactivity is reduced when the emotional process of the system shifts. That which maintains the shift is a changed identity.

Systems that are healthy and thus sustainable maintain stability by continuously changing. This idea grounds the theory in process. Learning is the ability not only to change but to continue to change as the world changes. Failing to change means certain death. This is true at a cellular level in the body, and it is true for the largest of organizations.

Finally, the fifth component of Systems Thinking is rooted in the principle of emergence. In systems, relationships are interdependent and mutually influential. Small changes in those relationships can result in large and profound differences over time. Systems are not open to being controlled. They are only open to being influenced. Disturbing any system will result in changes—some expected and some unintended. Watchfulness will allow the continuous adaptation that leads to sustainable health. Most systems have some feedback mechanism that allows for this change. People often choose to ignore the need for such observation and are constantly caught off guard.

There is an upside to this principle, however, which must be noticed. Significantly influencing a system does not require large movements but only nurturing conditions. Individually, learning is not about large changes in lifestyle but rather subtle changes in perception that lead very naturally to changed identity and changed behavior. As a leader, influencing others does not require you to be in complete control. Small changes in yourself or your organization can lead to very profound growth.

Conclusion

Discussion of this learning model has come full circle. The dynamic of change begins with Disturbances that grow into an awareness that is often experienced as Chaos. Letting Go of those things that inhibit your ability to influence and to be influenced creates space in which Learning can occur that results in increased awareness, intentionality, and coherence. Participating in this dynamic will result in a greater ability for differentiation. The greater the level of differentiation in the system, the more likely that the family, team, or organization will respond to anxiety more effectively and appropriately. Four core learning abilities—Emotional Awareness, Critical Reflection, Courage, and Systems Thinking—orient individuals to pay attention in such a way that they can more freely participate in the dynamic of Learning, rather than fight it. In the end, if there is any hope for a system based on freedom rather than fear, it will begin with individuals who are learning and maturing.

Chapter 6 - Opportunities for Leadership

"Leaders, apart from being able to manage themselves, show true leadership if they help others to manage themselves."
Manfred Kets de Vries – <u>Leaders, Fools and Impostors: Essays on the Psychology of Leadership</u>

If the process of learning and change is primarily a path from Disturbance through Chaos and Letting Go to a place of Learning, then leadership—the act of influencing the system— seeks to help individuals, teams and organizations continue to walk this path toward greater maturity and responsibility. This raises a critical question for leaders: Which doors provide access to facilitate the next possibility? This chapter identifies those critical concerns in each phase of the learning cycle that offer opportunities for leaders to take action so that others can begin their own maturing, self-differentiating process.

There is no single recipe for leadership. No approach or guideline will be effective in every situation. Too many variables influence the dynamic of learning. What is more helpful is to watch for opportunities a leader can use to help a group or individual toward learning. The four opportunities that can be useful in furthering individual and collective learning are Awareness, Clarity, Courageous Connection, and Curiosity (see Figure 6.1). There is no clear separation between these opportunities, however. One seeps into and overlaps the next.

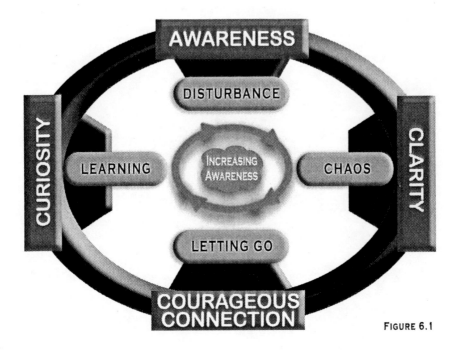

FIGURE 6.1

An important distinction must be made at this point: Leadership that promotes maturity in the entire system is always concerned with building the capacity of others as solutions are found and progress is made. For this reason, leadership can resemble good consulting. Good consultants help clients think clearly about the situations they are in and at the same time are adept at helping clients see options that were before unnoticed. In this sense, good consultants not only provide solutions but also help clients learn to think better or at least differently. Leaders should do much of the same. They should help those around them not only continue to make progress but to develop their learning abilities at the same time. As important as it is for leaders to take responsibility to differentiate themselves, if they can help others take those same steps, they are building organizations that will be sustainable.

Awareness

The initial steps of learning and change depend on an awareness of the need for learning and change. Thus, a critical leadership opportunity involves increasing the awareness of others. This begins with deep listening. Like was discussed in Chapter one, a leader must listen without and within. In beginning to *listen without,* "listen in particular for the degree of self-reflection in the questions [being asked by others]. To what extent . . . do they see their own part in what they are exploring? To what degree do they attribute their problems to sources outside themselves?"[1] Remember that an important result of increasing awareness includes helping others see the system of which they are a part as well as the system that they create and maintain by their choices.

Despite the importance of *listening without* to this process, *listening within* may be even more critical. Leaders are socialized to take action. Facilitating others toward learning does include action, but it grows out of waiting. There may be a strong desire to fix things or to get results. Instead, what others need at this point is help in asking important questions. Often, the first thing that comes to mind is only marginally relevant. Leaders must discern whether the first questions asked are seeking solutions and thus placing constraints on the interaction or are moving toward broadening others' perspectives. Good leaders wait to understand what is happening and why. This involves listening not just to the content but also to the process—that is, listening as much to what is not said as to what is said. Doing so requires paying attention to the internal emotional processes: 'What am I feeling, and what might that mean?' Then careful facilitation can lead to the awareness of things before not seen or considered. Listening within is to begin to listen to your own thoughts. Facilitating important questions with others requires that you first ask those questions of yourself.

There are at least two ways to facilitate awareness. First, a leadership influence might become a Disturbance in the system. This could occur by holding up a mirror of current reality for others to notice. This may or may not be an easy step, since acknowledging the current reality can be threatening. Isaacs suggests a continuum for facilitation that ranges from facilitate to name to engage.[2]

Facilitating learning conversations begins well before the actual conversation. It begins with creating conditions for openness and safety. Again, this can mean making sure there is enough space for others to encounter one another. Space is created by an uncluttered agenda. Too often, there are so many things to consider that the agenda is packed to the hilt. When this is the case, the anxiety of the group will grow. There will be no patience for careful consideration and learning. Space also comes from a facilitative leader who is centered and who has faith in the process.

Beyond creating conditions, facilitating means asking questions aimed at helping others pay attention to the process in which they are involved. A question like 'How well are things going?' will cause a group to step back and consider their process. Typically, groups are so engaged in their topic that they do not listen to the process.

At times, though, even the most carefully crafted question does not lead others to a new awareness. Naming is the next step. Naming can be thought of as making observations. I remember working with a group that was being careful about what they were saying. I asked them what that cautiousness might mean. My observation not only drew their attention but also gave them permission to talk about an underlying issue of some importance. They had just not found a way to get it on the table. A leader's timely observation can open communication greatly.

Naming as a way of creating awareness is to operationalize your own curiosity. Look beyond the obvious. What is being discussed is not necessarily the most important thing happening. Often, there are other things just below the surface. All that is needed is someone to be gently curious to bring them to the surface.

Engagement is the most assertive action on Isaacs continuum. When questions, conditions, and observations do not open the eyes of others, engagement is an attempt to enter the system and prompt the needed response. This is not simply modeling. The focus is not to get others to do anything directly. Instead, the focus is on the individual who is trying to be a learning, exploring, adventurous person among persons who have not reached such a point. Others may and often do learn how to be different simply because someone is different among them. This approach can be used when teaching groups to learn collectively. The leader does not have to worry about getting group members to ask good questions in the beginning. The leader simply asks those questions among them. Before too long, group members notice that they are asking different types of questions.

> *Facilitating learning conversations begins well before the actual conversation. It begins with creating conditions for openness and safety.*

Engagement requires caution, as well. If the facilitative leader enters too soon, the group will become dependent on him or her. If the facilitative leader enters and stays engaged too long, he or she will begin to drive the agenda, rather than those who are learning. And if the facilitative leader enters too late, it becomes difficult to repair the damage that has already occurred in the learning fabric. Once movement toward learning is noticed, the leader backs out and lets the group continue their journey.

Engagement is a willingness not to require of others what they cannot or will not give. It is an acceptance of what is. An engaging leader recognizes that others may not be able to see the path that would lead to a new way. By stepping out in front first, without requiring anything of others, the leader creates a space of extreme safety. The awareness of others will increase as the leader lives and works among them differently.

The other choice to facilitate awareness is for the leader to cajole, bait, seduce, or coerce others into his or her image of what should be. But the harder the leader pushes, the harder the group members resist. A negative, reactive cycle takes form. It should be noted that the leader's attempts at changing others are not motivated by malice. On the contrary, beneath the leader's actions is often an intent to help others succeed. There is a thin line between concern and compulsion, between love and violence. If the leader is not careful, his or her personal value will become entwined with the responses of others. "The result is a state of mind that makes us live as though our worth as human beings depends on the way others react to us."[3] Without a sense of transcendent meaning, it is easy to lose touch with a sense of purpose and value. It is from such a place that good intentions become wedges driven between people.

Before such thoughts are dismissed as irrelevant sentiments for serious leaders of organizations, consider how often in meetings those present blame the actions of others for why they cannot succeed. Engagement sees the limitations of others as secondary to the choices you choose to make for yourself. Rather than increase the distance between yourself and others who are vital to sustainable success, an effective leader closes the gap by choosing to live first what is desired in the other. Not only will this result in less resistance from others, but it will provide an opportunity to be surprised. If the only acceptable result is the preconceived one in your mind, you will not be able to see other manifestations of the ideal. Sustainable change usually comes in small steps of progress. If a leader does not let go of his or her own preconceived notions, he or she will never see the subtle changes that must be nurtured in order for others to mature into a new way of living.

Choosing to live differently among others can lead to another form of disturbance, which is to initiate the imagination of what might be. What is lived within is then articulated. This can take the form of sharing a vision that would include the description of the what and the why of a new possibility. Often, what determines who should lead in a particular setting is the ability to see what might be. For leaders who may *want* to disturb their organizations, this is a positive method of disturbance. Reframing an organization's purpose or future opportunities engages the aspirations of others. It also sets in motion a new cycle of learning.

Clarity

When the system is experiencing the chaos of change, it is difficult to move forward because the way is not clear. A leadership opportunity in a moment of chaos is to help others become clear about what is happening, what they may be feeling about that, and what they may need to let go of in order to move forward. This is a time when members of a system need to see more clearly the dynamics of that system. It is important that individuals become aware of how their own choices both create and sustain what they experience. They are not victims. Rather, they are all competent individuals who are not being intentional about their choices.

In addition to clarifying the contributions that all members make in keeping the system the same, leaders concerned with learning will help others become clear as to the assumptions being made. Recognizing assumptions is the key not only to changing behavior but also to changing what is noticed. Even though many tools can be employed, the following pages describe two: Emotional Chains and Polarity Maps.

> *A leadership opportunity in a moment of chaos is to help others become clear about what is happening, what they may be feeling about that, and what they may need to let go of in order to move forward.*

An Emotional Chain is a process that allows people to think systemically about their choices and behaviors by looking beyond the symptoms (behaviors) to their driving emotions and motivating beliefs.[4] By beginning to see that their choices are derived from the interaction of behavior, emotions, and beliefs, people can think at a level that allows them the depth to move toward understanding those unspoken mental models. Emotional Chains are created by sequentially mapping out people's emotions, their actions in response to their emotions, and the reactions of others to their actions (See Figure 6.2). After having created a sequential map of an experience, people can begin to ask the questions that will uncover the assumptions and beliefs behind the actions and emotions: What belief or assumption motivated your choice? What did that behavior do for you? What did you get out of that particular behavior? Individuals should think about the most basic and fundamental assumptions at this point. After they have some idea about what assumptions they were operating from, they can dispute these beliefs to see if they match reality and they can brainstorm other responses they could choose in light of this new perspective.

Here is an example from one of the author's own life. The context of this example was a peer-day meeting during my doctoral studies at the

Union Institute. There were four participants all together. However, it was my interaction with Michael that was a learning experience for me. See Figure 6.2 for the mapping of this Emotional Chain. The triggering event for me was Michael's confession that he was struggling with his vocation as pastor and was planning on leaving his church. I could resonate with his predicament since I had left professional ministry myself just a year previous. His alternative was to find solace within the theories of psychiatrist Carl Jung. As he began sharing his ideas, I noticed early on how uncomfortable I felt. I was experiencing an ever-increasing sense of anxiety. My first response to my discomfort was to provide a counterpoint to Michael's thoughts. He, of course, defended his position. I listened, but within, I was on edge. I made several more attempts to explain my point in such a way as to get him to reconsider his loss of faith. Each time, he defended his position. Eventually, I simply withdrew myself and limited my involvement in the conversation. I left the first half of this eight-hour session drained, uncomfortable, and very apprehensive about going back two days later for the remaining four-hour discussion.

I spent the days between sessions trying to connect my emotions and behavior to what underlying assumptions were giving rise to my state. I came to two conclusions. First, I realized that my behavior indicated that I, on some level, felt a responsibility to fix Michael's faith crisis. I was totally unable to hear him because I was too involved with attempting to heal and convert him. Each gesture of conversion was met with skepticism and a very articulate argument. My own sense of validation was completely enmeshed with his response to his faith. Letting go of this assumption allowed me to participate differently in the second session. Rather than try to get Michael to change his mind, I explored the path he had taken that had brought him to this place. My experience and his were similar in many ways. What I discovered was that although our solutions were very different, the questions we were asking were very similar. The second discovery I made from this chain is that I often require others to respond to situations as I would. Michael had clearly not come to the same conclusions about the church that I had. I had come to hold the institution in contempt. Michael had some doubts about the message. The root of this reactive response, it seems, may be that I fear I am not so far away from reaching the same conclusions he did. In addition, finding others who have the same response as I do validates my choices. The real key here was that I had crossed a boundary. My focus was on changing Michael, and I had no power or mandate to do that.

In the end, I decided to focus on myself and leave Michael to himself. In the next session, I explored the lives of my fellow learners, trying very hard to accept what was rather than remake things in my image. Consequently, I felt much more relaxed and in the end had a very good learning experience. This excerpt from my peer-day report summarizes the experience well:

> *I had another learning that was most unexpected but probably just as important as the ideas that have become clearer in this process. After the first day, I had an intense feeling of sadness. I was feeling somewhat alienated. Michael and I, although from similar backgrounds, had very different answers to our questions. At first I could not really figure out why I felt the heaviness. I am usually not a person who is so insecure that I must have everyone agree with me. After further review, I realized my melancholy seemed to come from the fact that these people had been failed by the faith that I hold so important. At first hearing, it seemed they could not figure God out so they were just grasping a worldview that did not require God. It was not until I was willing to let go of my need to "save" them that I could really enjoy the interaction. The second day was a much better experience because I was being responsible only for that which I am responsible for and no more. I trusted that each person would benefit from our gathering and would take what they needed.[5]*

As much as any amount of content, I learned and experienced a great deal in the process. I learned that although we are looking in quite different places, we each talked about the same source of pathology. This was encouraging. If four individuals with such different life experiences were naming the same things as a problem, we must be asking some very fundamental questions. Also, even though I did not agree with some of the solutions that were suggested as ways out of our current condition, I could dialogue with this group and learn from them. I was able to really practice something that I think is essential for a viable future. We must learn to listen to everyone. We need to explore their experience. Even if we never agree with the path to a better tomorrow, we all can benefit from the process of searching together if only for a brief while. It may be that in the searching we will find a way to be together in a much more healthy way.

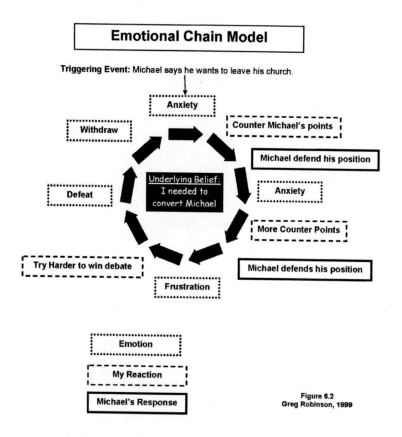

Figure 6.2
Greg Robinson, 1999

Clarity is essential to furthering the learning process. Certain situations tend to add confusion to the chaos. Often, members of systems get polarized around issues. Just as often, they get stuck because they do not recognize the underlying paradox of their issue. Resistance grows as one side, who clearly sees the answer, is exasperated by the other side, who are just as certain of their view. Their debate really has no resolution because each person thinks it is their side of the paradox that is the answer. There is no reason for either person to change their perspective since each side of the argument appears to be the opposite of the other party. Their lack of Clarity involves the very nature of how they are thinking about the issue. It is not one or the other that will result in sustainable success. Both are essential. Clarifying the points of each side will not resolve this. Only when both parties begin to see the nature of their disagreement can they move to a place where different perspectives can be appreciated. Johnson calls such paradoxes polarities.[6]

Polarities "are sets of opposites which can't function well independently. Because the two sides of a polarity are interdependent, you cannot choose one as a 'solution' and neglect the other".[7] Johnson lists several such polarities, including generic polarities such as the part and the whole, the self and the other, doing and being, change and stability, and unconditional respect and conditional respect. In sum, the critical ideas for Johnson's discussion of Clarity include recognizing the nature of polarities, the basic idea of managing polarities, and an approach to change utilizing the understanding of polarized systems.

As has been determined, polarities cannot be solved by choosing one extreme over the other. Over time, both are necessary for sustainability. Individuals will struggle until they let go of the need for simplistic certainty and accept the nature of paradox and the ambiguity it brings. In fact, in the fast-paced world of today, polarities emerge much more quickly. Consequently, the limitation of trying to choose one side to the exclusion of the other is exposed in short order.

A key to polarities is to realize they are not problems to solve but dilemmas to manage. Johnson provides a valuable mapping technique that helps expose the nature of polarities so that they can be managed which is the second tool of recognizing our assumptions.[8] The primary purpose of mapping a polarity is to understand that each side has an upside and a downside. You can begin to create a polarity map by taking a polarity and placing it on a continuum. Then above each end, describe the positive characteristics of that pole. Likewise, below each pole, describe its negative characteristics. The result is a quadrant map that will reveal the complete nature of the polarity.

Polarities have a perpetual flow dynamic that goes from the upside of one side to the downside of the same polarity. When the pain of the downside is great enough, relief will be sought in the upside of the other pole. A great example of this is to trace the pendulum swing from centralized to decentralized in organizational theory. Historically, organizations tend to move back and forth between a strong, centralized governance to a more decentralized system. Over time, each of these systems of governance has its downside. Rarely do organizational leaders think that the answer may be some combination of the two. Ultimately, the new "solution" of the upside of the chosen pole will itself lead to its own downside. Graphically, this can be depicted as an infinity loop. The secret for effective leaders to manage polarities is to first be able to see the entire polarity—the upsides and downsides of both poles. Next, it is important to recognize the warning signs of the downside so that balance can be sought in emphasizing those things that promote the upside of the opposite pole.

Self-differentiated leaders should consider a crucial polarity: ambition versus humility (Figure 6.3). The upside of ambition is the striving for progress and forward motion. Without such striving, it is easy to become stagnant. The downside of ambition is that the ends can come to justify the means. People are just resources to use or obstacles to overcome as you seek the goal at hand. Such practices undermine the trust necessary for any organization to succeed over time. The upside of humility is that you are always mindful of the responsibility that leadership brings. The well-being of others often depends on the decisions leaders make. Humility also keeps leaders centered so that the power available to them does not subvert their character. Individuals with too much humility will not take a stand when difficult circumstances require courage. There is no end to managing this polarity. Only constant vigilance and continuous learning will provide the necessary balance. Such mindfulness makes for great leaders.

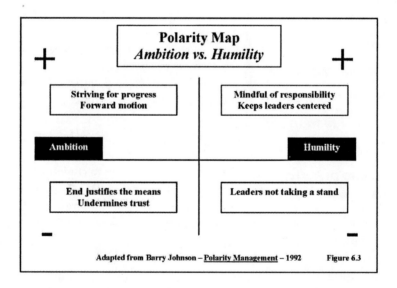

Polarity management provides one other critical piece of knowledge. Johnson talks of change associated with polarities in terms of crusaders and tradition bearers.[9] Basically, his theory is that in most situations, there are some individuals who are anxious for something new. They see the downside of the pole currently being emphasized and also see the upside of the opposite, balancing pole. These are crusaders. At the same time, there are others who see the benefits of the status quo along with the potential limitations of the opposite pole. Their fear is that the good of what is will be thrown out in an enthusiastic charge toward what might be. These are tradition bearers. Leaders who want to contribute to furthering the dynamic of learning in their organizations are wise to realize that both perspectives are right. Choosing to empower one over the other will only divide the organization and limit its capacity to deal with change in the future. In fact, such limited vision combines with the anxiety in the system to promote a quick-fix mentality.

A key to furthering change in such conditions is to make sure both sides see the whole polarity. However, you should begin with hearing the views of the tradition bearers. Doing so will calm their anxiety and encourage their listening to the crusader point of view. Crusaders, although impatient, will have the greater level of energy and will have no difficulty creating movement when the time comes. Helping others understand the paradoxical nature of organizations by mapping critical polarities develops a mature mindset. Such a mindset is the foundation of a sustainable learning organization.

> *Polarities have a perpetual flow dynamic that goes from the upside of one side to the downside of the same polarity.*

In addition to Emotional Chains and Polarity Maps, seeing your place in the system dynamics is another crucial area of Clarity. Each member of a system makes choices that perpetuate the nature and process of the system. Just as often, members do not see their individual contributions because they are too focused on seeing the contributions of others.

However, unless a critical mass within the organization begins to understand how their choices influence the whole, learning will remain a distant ambition. Creating such Clarity requires individuals who are open to seeing what is, but it is not a task that can be done alone. You cannot truly understand your role unless it is reflected back through interaction with others.

The critical mindset for such an exercise is one of taking personal responsibility. If this is not required by the leader/facilitator, the discussion will quickly devolve into finger pointing and blaming. Again, gentle but firm questioning that redirects the attention of individuals to themselves will empower a group to learn collectively.

Courageous Connection

Of the four leadership opportunities, Courageous Connection may be the one that most distinguishes true leaders. The other opportunities have a variety of tools and techniques that facilitate those actions. But Courageous Connection is an attitude, a mindset and a strength of will that faces the discomfort of change and learning in order to enter into real learning. It is the mindset that does not panic in the midst of chaos but can wait until order and meaning emerge.

Courageous Connection contains elements of presence, vulnerability, and potential loneliness. The greatest gift any leader can give to a group of followers is himself or herself. Being able to remain calm in the midst of elevated anxiety is essential to moving toward Learning. The tendency of the system is to be reactive. A nonanxious presence is provided by containing your own anxiety through self-awareness and self-regulation while staying connected in a real way to others who are trying to progress. To do so requires the ability to not react to other's reactivity. Often, leaders either seek to rescue those who seem to be experiencing discomfort or to distance themselves from those same people in order not to experience any discomfort themselves. Courageous Connection recognizes that at times of real transformation, leaders should remain closely connected and take the first step toward Learning. This going first—or living out what others need to do in order to learn—requires would-be leaders to be vulnerable. A spirit of adventure is essential and it may feel lonely for a while. This takes patience. In terms of the dynamics of the system, others may borrow from the leader's will until they develop their own confidence to let go.

This presence was a critical component of what made Phil Jackson so successful as a leader. Here is how Michael Jordon describes Jackson's presence:

> With Doug [Collins, former coach] you could always feel the tension, while Phil was poised at all times. Doug was more emotional. He wasn't afraid to show you exactly how he was feeling. As a player you connect with the atmosphere the coach creates. With Phil it was like we were in harmony with each other in the heat of battle. We were comfortable not only with each other but also with the situation no matter how difficult the moment. We were able to find peace amid the noise, and that allowed us to figure out our options, divine solutions and be clear-headed enough to execute them. That's what Phil Jackson brought to the Chicago Bulls and that's what we all connected with.[10]

What many leaders do not recognize is that most groups in organizations do not need a leader to tell them what to do. This creates dependency and works against maturing an organization to handle the difficulties of life. The leader's greatest gift is presence which creates the emotional space to calm rampant anxiety and allow organization members to think clearly. The solutions will undoubtedly follow.

Curiosity

If learning is essentially a process of increasing awareness, intentionality, and coherence, then being curious provides a tremendous opportunity to promote learning. Being curious may include seeking to learn from experience (to be reflective), to expand the current understanding of an issue or situation by uncovering assumptions, or to invite an expansion of perception through the sharing of diverse perspectives. In the process, a new sense of meaning will emerge within individuals and among system members. Fragmented thoughts can become coherent in this context of shared inquiry.

The attitude of Curiosity is predicated on an understanding of the relationship between leadership and communication. If leaders are to influence and perpetuate the learning process, three factors will determine the success of their communication: direction, distance, and anxiety.[11]

> **Curiosity promotes patient listening, rather than hurried activity; consideration, rather than quick solutions; and intentionality, rather than reactivity.**

Direction refers to the notion that "people can only hear you when they're moving towards you. As long as you are in the pursuing or rescuing position, your message will never catch up".[12] Curiosity is a manifestation of non-pursuit. Rather than force ideas on others, leaders invite others to come together when they explore not only the positions of others but also the reasoning behind such positions. Asking questions, probing the experience and thinking of others, is a collaborative action that promotes reciprocal inquiry by others. Although Curiosity may appear simply to be an asking of questions, it represents a tremendous shift in the emotional process of the system. Curiosity promotes patient listening, rather than hurried activity; consideration, rather than quick solutions; and intentionality, rather than reactivity. Such actions reflect a participation in the learning dynamic.

Being curious is in contrast to pursuing others in conversation. Pursuit results when you cross the boundary from making observations to requiring those listening to see as you do. A manifestation of pursuit I have noticed in groups is when one person makes a point and continues to repeat himself or herself in an attempt to get agreement from others. In the name of communication, learning is subverted as certainty becomes more important than inquiry.

Leaders cannot be curious and distant at the same time. *Distance* is the second important concept in understanding the emotional process of communication. Leaders who are too close smother those around them. They crowd others, thereby amplifying anxiety. Such leaders micromanage each detail. They can overanalyze even insignificant situations. On the other hand, leaders who are too far away promote anxiety. Remember that the leader's ability to know and regulate himself or herself is what promotes learning. A leader must have regular contact with those he or she would influence. This can be difficult if you fear vulnerability. This is one of the critical first steps that leaders are required to make. Again, others will not hear a leader if they are not moving toward him or her. Thus, distancing yourself from uncomfortable individuals or situations will not allow communication to be authentic or seen as valid. 'Do as I say, not as I do' is not a philosophy that will work in the arena of learning.

Tied very closely to the factors of distance and direction is *anxiety*. As discussed earlier in this book, learning will be inhibited unless leaders can refrain from reacting to the reactions of others. Leaders who can manage their own anxiety will not be seduced into rescuing others nor will they amplify the anxiety of others. They will not attempt to over-control the situation.

Conclusion

Over time, Curiosity will undoubtedly lead to the next Disturbance. One other component of Curiosity is the continuous search to understand the larger environment, and the possible effects it may have on the system are important. As learners become comfortable at exploring their own experience, they will develop the skills and courage to engage the larger environment. Each time around the learning path expands individuals' awareness and can engage them in ever-greater conversation with the world they inhabit. With each learning encounter, people develop a greater capacity not to panic in periods of chaos but rather to explore them as opportunities for growth.

Case Overview

The following chapter deals with a leader who is seeking to embed self-differentiated leadership and learning in the culture of his start-up organization. This attempt challenges the long held mindset of employees that look for others to tell them what to do. For his organization to be successful, employees will have to transform themselves into leaders able to determine their own direction while providing solutions for their customer's success. This story examines one process for developing self-differentiated leaders at all levels of the organization. If the theory is to be useful, it must be transferable. The account of this technology start-up reveals both the successes and difficulties in facilitating and sustaining differentiated learning.

Chapter 7 - Creating a Learning Culture

"I believe life consistently improves for humanity over time, but it does so only because individuals, communities, and nations take it upon themselves not only to imagine a future worth creating, but actually trying to build it."
Thomas Barnett - <u>The Pentagon's New Map</u>

There is another significant question yet to be answered: If leadership is an ongoing process of Learning, with the desired destination of self-differentiation, can that process be taught? A model that allows us to conceptualize something is still a far cry from making those concepts useful in the real world. If this model of leadership can be taught, can it also create organizational practices that actually embed this way of thinking in how an organization works?

If the answer to any of these questions is yes, then: How is this leadership and organization development done? And how long will it take? In the swirling conditions of change, there is a critical need for leaders not only to pursue their own learning and change but to develop organizational cultures that facilitate the same maturing process in others.

This chapter chronicles one case of a newly developed internal IT (Information Technology) Consulting Company that intentionally set out to create a culture of continuous learning and leadership. Whereas the Safety group described in the next chapter sought to change a cross-functional work group, this project looked to embed an ongoing learning process in an intact work group. In addition to describing the organizational conditions that gave rise to this experiment, time lines, goals, and observable results, this chapter will explore the insights of members of this organization as they shifted their own mindsets to become self-differentiated professionals. Appendix B includes portions of an interview with the leader, Brent Coussens, of this radical change initiative. This organization's story highlights an organic approach to change. The idea of leadership as self-differentiation guided both the process and the desired result of this organization's journey.

Humble Beginnings

The IT Consulting Company (CC) began as an idea that grew to a reality when there was a reorganization. One of the business units decided not to have their own internal IT professionals. Consequently, they consolidated offices and decided to outsource most of the IT work. The CC began when the displaced workers from the reorganization and another existing group came together to start something new. What is even more remarkable about this story is that these were people who had just survived a downsizing. It would not be unreasonable to think that morale may not have been at an all-time high. Beginning a brand-new experiment in the wake of such a dramatic chain of events had an added perception of risk.

With only a small band of willing pioneers, the leadership set a course for a new beginning. They did not have a complete master plan. What they did have was a clearly articulated vision of what they believed was necessary to thrive and the willingness to experiment. One of the authors was asked to come in and assist them in being very intentional about establishing a culture in which there was a high level of personal responsibility and self-determination. Above all else, members of this organization needed the capability to change continuously and adapt as the organizational context changed. The leadership bet the future on developing the ability for everyone to learn both individually and collectively.

It should also be mentioned that most of the rest of the organization were very skeptical about this experiment. Many were fearful that the experiment would end badly and that those who were employed by the CC would be left without positions.

Goals

The CC began with several goals. A critical goal for the larger organization was that this new organization would allow them to improve efficiency and thus reduce the cost for the IT services that the company needed. The financial target for the first nine months was to have one or two months in which the CC broke even.

Additionally, the CC asked its members to transform themselves from traditional IT professionals, who performed a specific function, to consultants, who anticipate the needs of their clients and provide solutions to their client's dilemmas. This would require a tremendous shift in mindset for everyone. There would be a greater level of responsibility and expectation of each individual not only to understand the technology but to have interpersonal skills that would allow them to influence others. CC members would be expected to think and to help the organization make the best decisions possible. They would have to take responsibility for their own learning and development. There would be plenty of opportunity for learning, but there would be no manager to mandate choices for them.

A third goal was to develop a culture that promoted continuous learning, self-determination, and strong leadership at all levels. The ability to learn was believed critical for success. The leadership team often talked of developing "Navy Seal–type" employees, who could be placed in any situation and figure out how to add value.

The Intervention

The intent of the intervention was really threefold: First, the leadership team wanted to create a certain mindset. They wanted to influence the way CC members thought about themselves, their work, and their customers. They wanted them to think of learning as something more than gathering information. They suggested that learning—that is, the ability to create sustainable change—would call for three things: an increase in the awareness of the assumptions people held; an increased intentionality, in which there would be less reactivity; and a greater amount of purposeful choosing which would develop a broader perspective. They wanted members to be able to collaborate with their colleagues and their customers. There would be a tremendous need for CC members to be open to influence and to be willing to influence others. A final component of the mindset was the willingness for CC members to take personal responsibility for their work and their future. In addition, the leadership team asked them to write a learning agreement. This would be a plan that would spell out the prior learning that they brought with them to the CC, what they needed to learn to become the IT consultants they needed to become, and how they would gain the knowledge necessary to be successful.

The second intention was to embed opportunities for members to meet regularly. These opportunities would be intentional times set aside to reflect, question, and learn both individually and collectively. The primary opportunities were to be action-learning meetings, which would occur every two to four weeks. These meetings would be continued after the formal intervention had been completed as a mechanism to encourage meaningful interaction. In these small groups of three to six members, the mindset would be practiced and new skills of reflection, openness, and shared learning would be cultivated.

The third intent of the intervention was to teach a process for learning collaboration. The leaders' belief was that an intentional process was needed for the action-learning teams to follow. They did not want the opportunities for connection to be without purpose. This process of action learning is not new, but it provides a disciplined way of interacting so that collaboration and individual responsibility are allowed and encouraged. The process involves each member bringing an issue or problem that he or she is facing. Now, this issue or problem should not be interpreted solely as something negative. It could be something that had gone very well but that the individual who was presenting wanted to look at more closely so as to understand why things had worked so well. The criteria for a good issue or problem included that

> **Action learning provides a disciplined way of interacting so that collaboration and individual responsibility are allowed and encouraged.**

it must be real; it must have meaning to the person or organization; it must be something within the direct influence of the presenting individual, and it must have no known answer.

The group then helps their colleague do two things. First, by asking good questions, they make sure the presenter is addressing the real, root issue. Too often, solutions are sought without thinking if the right problem is being solved. Second, the group brainstorms with the presenter for possible solutions or strategies for addressing the issue. The presenter's responsibility is to bring something to the group and to take action on what is discussed in the meeting. Then, in the next meeting, the presenter reports back to the group on how his or her actions went. Although simple in nature, the process provided enough structure for the groups to have purposeful, focused interaction.

Organic Change

Even though it is much clearer now in hindsight, this was truly an organic approach to change. The focus was not to define sequential prescribed steps but rather to create the right conditions that would allow success to be amplified and fear to be overcome. The leadership did not know for sure how this experiment would turn out, but they had a clear picture of the goal or result they were trying to attain. By choosing a method that was consistent with the result, the stage was set to let things start small and grow naturally.

Having a clear vision of the desired future guided the creation of conditions, expectations, and practices that would make it easier to pursue that vision. In addition, by focusing on conditions, they did not force everyone to begin or arrive at the same time. Each person started this journey from a different point and moved at his or her own speed. Nevertheless, the practices of the organization and leadership continued to influence the CC members toward the vision.

Time Line

Figure 7.1 is an overview of the project's timeline. The leadership team began with the idea that it might take six to nine months before the learning process took full root. As it turned out for this group, nine to ten months was needed to make the teams self-sufficient. Since then, they have reorganized the learning teams due to growth. Theoretically, having the right mindset (i.e., the ability to lead and define themselves, rather than trying to change others) should allow them to form teams more quickly. After a few weeks in the new teams, that is exactly what began to happen.

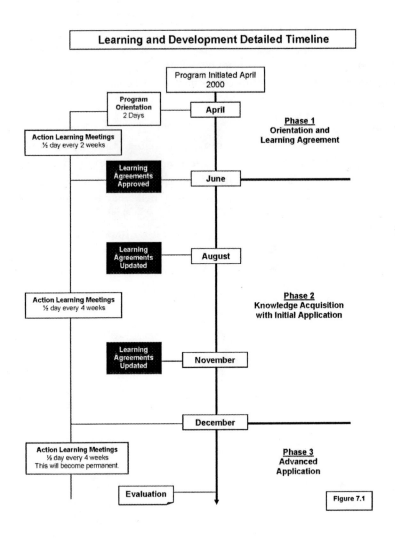

Learning and Development Detailed Timeline

Program Initiated April 2000

Program Orientation 2 Days

April

Phase 1
Orientation and
Learning Agreement

Action Learning Meetings
½ day every 2 weeks

Learning Agreements Approved

June

Learning Agreements Updated

August

Action Learning Meetings
½ day every 4 weeks

Phase 2
Knowledge Acquisition
with Initial Application

Learning Agreements Updated

November

December

Action Learning Meetings
½ day every 4 weeks
This will become permanent.

Phase 3
Advanced
Application

Evaluation

Figure 7.1

Observable Results

Financially, the CC far surpassed expectations. Not only did they break even, but they actually made $100,000 profit on $1.2 million in revenue. While many things allowed this success, according to the leadership, the influence of the culture should not be overlooked. It was important to have the right people. However, "once you have somebody in the group or once the group is established . . . [you] must have the means to actually increase their attitude and aptitude" (interview with manager).

A second factor in this success was that a culture of openness, learning, and mutual influence had been established. For certain, more time would be required to judge whether the culture and mindset can be sustained. But after one year, a collective curiosity and confidence arose among individuals who bought into the fact that collaboration, although a social process, was actually the result of changing oneself rather than others. One team member described the group's growth this way:

"We started as a new group of individuals that, on the surface, had little in common. Our only direct tie was the fact that we were members of the Consulting Company. A few had worked together on another project. Now, we have a stronger relationship that is not based on 'what we do' but on 'how we relate' to each other."

Another member reported:

"I felt our team went through a period of uncertainty where we did not understand the action-learning process. We did not know how to respond and act toward each other to create the desired results. Now, a great deal of trust has developed as our team has shared experiences with each other using the action-learning format. We have learned to listen and ask questions and challenge each other to think about things in a different way. This trust has overflowed and has assisted us outside our meetings where we can approach each other individually for advice."

A third sign of success was the acceptance of the CC by others in the organization. Whereas in the beginning, people tried to avoid the CC, now they are trying to join it. Consequently, the strong culture has allowed management to be selective about new hires, thus making it easier to perpetuate the culture by hiring people that can thrive in the CC.

It is important to realize how these results were achieved. Although this was not a scientific study and the results cannot be generalized beyond this group, the strategy for achieving organizational health and subsequently financial performance was based solely on the critical paradox that is the subject of this book. A good collective process was developed by focusing on equipping individuals to change themselves. The emphasis from the beginning was to let go of needing to change others to make oneself more comfortable; rather, the goal was to find ones security in having the ability to define his or her own stance and to choose his or her responses, rather than focusing on trying to change others.

The Bigger Question

There is a bigger question not yet asked in relation to this book's subject matter and this particular case study: Is there any evidence that individuals can develop the capacity to think differently, challenge assumptions, and begin to master the emotional process so crucial to healthy systems?

Seven months into establishing the learning-based culture, members of the CC who had been active in the action-learning process were surveyed. Out of the fifteen surveys distributed, there were eight responses. As a part of the survey, two questions were asked that are critical to the current topic:

- Has your awareness of your emotional process changed? If so, how?
- Has your awareness of your thinking process (including your assumptions) changed? If so, how?

Again, it would be difficult to generalize any of the findings beyond the individuals in the group. However, there may still be some lessons worth learning in their responses.

Initial observations of members' responses were that increasing the awareness of both thinking and emotional process was possible. For this group, the purposeful interactions within the learning teams encouraged more critical observation of inner processes. Seven of the eight respondents indicated increased awareness of their thinking processes. Four of the eight indicated increased awareness of their emotional processes.

Despite these reports of increased awareness, the leaders were unsure as to the level of proficiency developed in only seven months. Consider the following comments from members:

"My assumptions have begun to change—at least my awareness that they ever existed in the first place."

"I know I still make assumptions; [they] are so ingrained that I don't even realize it. But I am more aware of this now. At least sometimes, I do challenge my assumptions of others. Still, I need an outsider to shed light on assumptions."

The emotional process is more difficult. There is something more ingrained about the emotional process. Again, like thinking, the first step seems to be to an increased awareness that an emotional process is active:

"I am aware of my tendency to be defensive—trying to persuade others to my way of thinking. I have learned to stop myself and ask: 'What are the reasons driving those defensive feelings?'"

"Yes, in the heat of the moment, I don't consciously map through the Emotional Chains cycle. However, I now find myself reflecting on my reactions and responses later and questioning their basis."

"It is starting to change. At first, it was difficult to look at an issue and examine my feelings around that issue. I have noticed that when certain emotions are invoked, I have started to explore why I am feeling what I am feeling. This process has occurred subtly, and I am not sure when I started doing it."

Learning to pursue self-differentiated leadership is a long journey. In seven months, this group showed only the first steps. Awareness is critical, as is having some model or language to make meaning of the experience. But there is more to leadership than awareness. Even so, the group had shown some promising results. With only modest development in self-awareness, the group created a culture that supported and demonstrated openness to influence. Even the slightest increases in intentionality and patience had a dramatic effect on the organization.

A Leader's Perspective

In bringing this chapter to a close, we want to highlight portions of an interview (see full interview in Appendix B) with the manager of this group to demonstrate how the pursuit of a learning based culture where differentiated leadership is the desired result requires particular things of a leader. To achieve this transformation, the leader extends the transformation he or she is experiencing within to the conditions that the remainder of the organization experience. By understanding the role of Disturbance and Letting Go, a leader can promote not only a new attitude but a new way of thinking. Such a leader will continue to seek to bring awareness and clarity to the members of the organization. In staying connected and taking courageous action, a leader can develop a culture where those willing to risk responsibility and further development will take their first steps. Consequently, the leadership tasks are more concerned with establishing a context or container for Learning than in giving direct orders as to how to work.

> **To truly disturb a system the leader must be willing to let go and take a risk.**

For our leader Brent, his first step was to act as a Disturbance to the new organization. He began with a very different concept of his organization. His vision was to create a very collaborative environment where people took responsibility for co-creating their work, their culture and their organization. It would be a fluid organization based on roles that anyone could play assuming they took the responsibility to be competent to play the role. This began the development of a new mindset. A little less than a year into it and there were signs of the Disturbance taking hold:

> *"People have bought into the sense of being, so to speak—of "What do I want this to be?" The majority of the people have bought into "I can help shape that round thing into what I want it to be." I think in a fairly short time, a short time being less than a year, that we have created an identity."*

To truly disturb a system the leader must be willing to let go and take a risk. Disturbance in a living system is not just a new set of orders. It sets in motions multiple consequences many of which are not even intended. It is the courage that grows out of conviction that will allow a leader to set the stage for an organization to grow. Brent talked about this process as a "leap of faith".

> *"It takes a step of faith. You have to be able to go out and get on the end of the limb. You don't have to understand everything about how it is going to take place, meaning that you don't have to know from A to Z what the order might end up being. In fact, I don't think that you can anyway. Having somebody that knows more about it than you is really important. We have leveraged you [one of the authors] for this…"*

As a Disturbance grows into awareness in a system, there is a tremendous need to help bring Clarity to the emerging Chaos. In this organization, there was an initial excitement about the possibility of the new vision, but how that would be accomplished was really not very clear. Brent demonstrated how a leader can take advantage of this critical opportunity to lead. Clarity is not micro-managing. Rather it is establishing enough boundaries and processes so that people involved in the organizational transformation can have some sense of stability. Brent did this by creating just a few simple rules that would guide the organization.

> *"The only thing that I would even consider a new idea in my mind was the action-learning teams. And that was really formalizing a concept. I think that is really what we have done; we have formalized some of this.*

Everybody knows that you want to have the right kind of culture in a group. But how many people actually assign somebody to say part of your responsibility is the culture, 'King of Culture.' We have been deliberate in some of those efforts."

Maintaining the momentum once a new culture is taking place is the next challenge for a leader. The new culture will only mature over time and that will require that a leader be able and willing to do at least three things: 1) be curious, always be learning themselves and adapt when necessary, 2) be patient, wait and do not bolt at the first sign of trouble and 3) be transparent—allowing others to see the process not just the outcomes will develop maturity and judgment.

These characteristics are shown in how Brent continued to reflect on the experience of his new organization:

"When we got started, there was a lot of excitement around it. We did a few things up front to help bring these two partial groups into one. We immediately hired some other people. There was a level of excitement there for the first month or two. I thought we had momentum on our side; things were rolling. We went through a period of two or three months where we weren't really paying attention to some of the culture stuff. We initiated it, we put it out there, but we weren't really measuring it (measuring in a nonquantitative way). All of a sudden, we lost the momentum and it started going back down the hill."

There are always those individuals who though they like the idea, will be cautious to commit until they see results. Brent's organization was no exception. It was his willingness to make the new endeavor transparent (a manifestation of courageous connection) that has allowed others to grow in their confidence in the organizational concept.

"They wanted to know if we were really going to follow through with this. And I think we have. I think they are also looking for how transparent the leader is. When things are good, do you say they are good? When things are not good, do you say, 'Hey, we need to do something here?' We are a very transparent organization, I feel."

Conclusion

Attempting an organizational transformation is not easy. In fact it is wrought with many potential pitfalls and opportunities for failure. The "pearl of great price" that a leader may find is an empowered workforce who not only does quality work, but who are changing themselves and thus a piece of the world as they go. Leaders will find many unexpected companions in this journey. But the journey will only be a possibility without the courage to take the first step.

Case Overview

Differentiated leaders do not rely on authority to force change. They realize this is a momentary success at best. They also recognize that to truly change the organization the members must be willing to change themselves. Consequently, a critical responsibility of differentiated leadership is creating the conditions and opportunities for others to change themselves as they redefine how they want to work with others. Differentiated leaders recognize that sustainable change is the result of a learning process and as such pursues organizational change from a learning based change perspective.

In the following chapter, change is considered from this perspective. Rooted in differentiated learning, a leader steps out first and reveals a path to a brighter tomorrow. This leader attempts to shift a fearful safety organization where members are disconnected into a coherent organization that is guided by a common set of guiding principles. This represents a fundamental shift in the organization's culture.

Chapter 8 - The Anatomy of a Successful Learning-Based Change Initiative

"If the world is saved, it will not be saved by old minds with new programs but by new minds with no programs at all."
Daniel Quinn - <u>Beyond Civilization</u>

If there is one phrase that captures the essence of what this book is about, it is the above quote. A fundamental paradox underlies good leadership. This paradox is not another, more clever example of how to get people to do what you want. That is an old mentality, and an abundance of programs already out there can develop your technique. New minds conceive of leadership as something much more. New minds understand the contribution of leadership is not to get others to do the bidding of leaders but to equip others to conceive of their circumstance and even their purpose in a different light. The health of society's institutions is interconnected with the ability of leaders to define themselves. This self-definition creates a fundamental shift in the emotional process of the organization. Rather than remain captive to the way things have always been done, the influence of a self-differentiated leader is to create enough courage in the system to tolerate the discomfort of learning a new way of functioning.

This chapter explores the experience of one small change initiative involving the Safety/Loss Control organizations within a large, established Fortune 500 company. It will describe the organizational context that stimulated this action along with the philosophy of learning-based change that guided their effort. Their story will include timelines (see figure 8.3 at the end of this chapter), a description of observable results, and portions of an interview with the leader of this effort. Paul, the corporate director of Health, Safety, and Environmental Affairs, brought one of the authors into this project in April 1999, because of my position as organizational consultant. My role was to give advice on how to make critical changes to the way this portion of the organization functioned and to create a process that would facilitate those changes. Along with Paul, a member of the audit group acted as a liaison between our change team and the audit committee.

Organizational Context

The setting for this project was a well established energy company. As noted in Chapter six, this company was a company with over 12,000 employees. The company had three platforms of business. The oldest business is in regulated natural gas pipelines. In addition, the company had a group of non-regulated energy businesses that included everything from fuel refineries to convenience stores. The third and fastest-growing business was the Energy, Marketing and Trading group.

This company had, like all companies, been influenced by societal changes. In a 1998 leadership study in partnership with a prominent consulting firm, a clear statement of intent was defined. Namely, the company would attempt to balance the need for speed that comes from autonomous units with the maximum efficiency that results from economies of scale. Consequently, there was a shift away from the tradition of the company being a holding company to one of a company with an integrated enterprise mindset.

One element that was not so quick to change was the form of the organization. Although the intent was to have collaboration between autonomous units, the organization was still wrestling with its legacy of autonomous hierarchies organized around functions. This proved to be a major hurdle to overcome. However, for a company to gain the speed and flexibility necessary for success in this age, a newer form had to emerge that made it easier for all to see the big picture yet make local decisions.

The Beginnings of Change

The impetus for the Safety/Loss Control change initiative came in the form of an external audit of the company's safety practices. An item of particular importance was the lack of formal linkage between at least thirteen different groups managing loss-control issues across the organization, resulting in a fragmented effort. Information was difficult to obtain. There was no way to provide assurance of the effectiveness of the organization as a whole to achieve its objective of "protecting the public, the environment, and our natural resources by operating in a safe, reliable manner".[1]

The mandate of the project was to implement a common management system for safety and loss control across the organization. In addition, the objective was to create a greater ability and willingness to share information across functional groups. Like many corporate mandates, this one came with no formal authority to reorganize or change reporting relationships. As it has turned out, this was a gift, for it forced the group to look for more creative solutions. The task would be daunting. We were operating in the wake of years of business unit autonomy that had promoted a lack of coordination and trust. We were also following several years of cross-enterprise change initiatives that had, by then, gained an infamous reputation.

A Learning Approach to Organizational Change

From the beginning, Paul and I were determined to learn from the plethora of authority-based change activities already in motion in the organization. As we began to devise a plan, we began to think first about the differences in the nature and makeup of a learning-based change initiative compared to the traditional model (see figure 8.1). Second, there were different priorities for the process of change. Finally, if the change were to be sustainable, we would need to create the right conditions to nurture and support the new change.

	Authority Based Change	Learning Based Change
Structure	Hierarchy	Networks
Primary Goal	Control	Learning
Primary Tactic	Power	Trust and communication
Sustained By	Compliance	Learning and adapting
Changed By	Imposed from outside	Emerges from interaction
Basic Trait	Rigid	Flexible
Cost	Initially quicker, but more resistance in the end	Initially slower, but with less resistance in the end

Figure 8.1

The primary instruments of an authority approach to change are a strong hierarchy, perceived power, and a relentless persistence. A small group of leaders get together and decide on "the answer" for the organization's circumstances. They then set out to create "buy-in" to their ideas. Their effort will be sustained by the continued compliance of the rest of the organization. Because attempting to change an organization of any size takes a long time, the effort can be derailed in a myriad of ways. Consequently, a change management plan is often devised to limit all signs of variance. The result is often a very rigid organization. Initially, such change efforts are quicker, but they ultimately create more resistance. Some research indicates that only about 30 percent of change initiatives succeed. The price of authority-based change is a quick start and a slow death.

Learning-based change has a completely different form. It finds life in networks, in which trust and communication are high and learning is the desired outcome. Rather than begin with "the answer," learning-based change begins with good questions. It is assumed that many answers may be needed. Those answers emerge from interaction among the organization's members, as they seek to understand their current issues from new perspectives. The underlying belief is that the only change efforts that truly succeed are those that increase the capacity of the organization to continue to learn and adapt in the future. No matter how good an idea may be today, it will be obsolete someday and the organization will need the ability to find the next necessary step. One perceived limitation of learning-based change is that it is too slow. In addition, it requires high levels of interpersonal skill. Another criticism is that the "soft stuff" just gets in the way of progress. The truth is that because change is not imposed from the outside but rather discovered in the process of learning together, there is little resistance in the end.

As the leaders of this change effort, we summoned great courage and insight to choose the sustainable path. We believed our continued success lay in the ability to induce change, rather than impose it. We set out on a journey that, from the beginning, had different priorities.

Even though the temptation was to do the easy work first—namely, to change structure and titles—we knew that was an illusion. We could have attempted to muster support for reorganization in order to consolidate power and give it to a single leader. But even if such an attempt had been achieved, we would have alienated the rest of the safety groups. Sharing information and enforcing the "right way" would have been a never-ending battle.

So, our first priority was to change the *mindset* of the groups. Working with a small group of the functional managers from each safety group, our success would lie in changing the way these managers interacted. They had lived in an environment of autonomy and mistrust for years. If the safety function were to achieve a new and integrated form, the leaders of those organizations would be required to embrace a new way of working. They would never be able to conceive of a new way if they could not learn to interact without posturing, debating, and resisting each other. That type of interaction was bred in the competitive world of an enormous hierarchy and could only create more of the same.

We kicked off the change initiative by gathering the relevant functional managers. We spent the first half day trying to describe a new way of talking together. Our objective was to develop the capacity to learn collectively. Collective learning seeks to develop a broader and more complete perspective through dialogue and inquiry. Rather than prove who had the best way, we wanted the group to develop the ability to challenge their assumptions and create an atmosphere in which differences were explored, rather than stamped out. It would require members who could develop high levels of self-awareness and self-regulation in order to transform the nature of the group's interaction. In addition, the managers would have come to think of leadership as changing themselves and influencing others rather than being right and in charge. We used the learning model introduced in Chapter three to frame the mindset that would be needed.

While they were not enthusiastic, the group did agree with the premise of learning-based change. The next challenge would be to change the group's

> *A change management plan is often devised to limit all signs of variance. The result is often a very rigid organization. Initially, such change efforts are quicker, but they ultimately create more resistance.*

practice. Even if they had completely internalized the ideas of collective learning, they had a long history of habits that served them well as they attempted to protect their turf and win their point. Asking questions, self-awareness, and critical reflection were things that did not come naturally. It was painful at first. The conversation was dominated by debate, hypersensitivity, and frustration. However, by the second day, the beginnings of interactions that promoted learning had taken root. True to the theory, the group did better work in less time. The first day, they had spent nearly two hours debating one principle. On the second day, they worked through nine more principles and planned the next meeting in less than five hours. They left early.

Learning-based change recognizes that if we can think differently, we can begin to act differently. New possibilities, before unseen, emerge in the space of intent listening and active trust. Changed behavior is the desired outcome of any learning effort, but changing the actions does not mean change has occurred. Sustainable change comes from the inside out.

Once a new mindset has been accepted and practices become consistent with the newly adopted mindset, a new culture can emerge. As groups within an organization reflect together on their practices, a new, shared meaning arises. In fact, the very act of reflection develops the skill necessary to continue to allow that culture to remain vital and adaptive over time. A critical component of the change initiative for the Safety/Loss Control group was to intentionally reflect on their practices. By examining together what was working well and what was not working so well, both in their safety programs and their group process, a new culture emerged among the leaders. Rather than avoid each other, they came together and learned to share knowledge. Not only was information shared, but the new mindset of collective learning led them to share their assumptions and thinking processes, as well. They were becoming smarter together than they were alone.

Our small group had decided on a different form of change initiative. Rather than force change, we sought to make it a learning process. We entered the process with the foundational priorities aligned. However, one more piece would determine how sustainable this effort would be. We needed to embed an infrastructure (see figure 8.2) that would create and support conditions conducive to collaboration and organizational learning. The architecture of this collaborative infrastructure would include attitude, opportunity, process, and a catalyst.

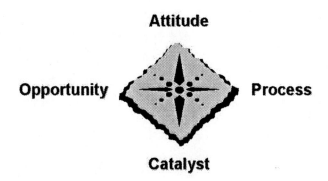

FIGURE 8.2

Attitude

Attitude refers to the way individuals see the world. It is the mindset that defines how members of the organization will interact and accomplish their work. For the safety professionals, changing their attitude meant first getting to know their colleagues. It also meant learning to interact differently. Again, this group used the learning model presented earlier in this book to define the type of interactions they were pursuing. No longer could this group be dominated by reactive and defensive debate driven by individuals who feared that others would discover their imperfections. We sought to develop their leadership skills to a point where they possessed the inner strength to not panic during the Chaos of learning a new attitude and the facilitative skill to invite others to risk asking important questions.

Purpose and *guiding principles* are also critical components of attitude. They form the shared understanding of what the organization is about and how each person will pursue that purpose. They also act as a stabilizing force that allows for high levels of cohesive action yet protects the need for autonomy. Principles are not prescriptive, in that they define specifically what each person will do; rather, they help to prioritize actions and act as criteria in decision making. Over time, purpose and principles are enduring. They act to define the identity of the team.

Principles were a critical component of the safety group's new organization. Remember, their original goal was to implement a common management system across groups that served very diverse business units. The businesses that this group supported ranged from a refinery in Alaska to natural gas pipelines in the Gulf of Mexico to convenience stores in Tennessee. There was little hope of finding one way to do all this work. The solution was a set of guiding principles that everyone could use to guide their work. These were not policies or procedures. Instead, they were principles that defined what was important in a good safety program. Each business would find different methods to manifest the safety principles, but looking over all the safety groups, there would be a set of common factors to which all would adhere.

The principles provided a common language around which the safety managers could learn. Each session, they took one or two of the principles and talked about how each was applying the principle to his or her area. In addition, discussing the principles allowed an atmosphere of trust to emerge. These principles allowed for the autonomy and flexibility that each manager would need. The principles also allowed a clear sense of cohesion for those within the safety organization and those business leaders looking in from the outside.

Opportunity

Opportunity is the second piece of the infrastructure. If change is to be effective, members of the organization require opportunities to interact. Too frequently, organizations spend time defining new ways of working together but allow the new vision to die because it goes neglected after the initial offsite meeting. Teams that struggle are fragmented and lack enough opportunities for connection to remained aligned and allow new learning to take place. We built into the change process ongoing opportunities for the safety managers to continue and build on what they had begun. They came together once a quarter for two days. After a year and a half, the core purpose of the meetings remained to learn.

Process

Having regular meetings is not unusual in organizations. What is it that made these opportunities so successful? Within the opportunities, there was a clearly defined process, the third piece of the infrastructure. Understanding the process of collective functioning, recognizing what is occurring, and having some ability to influence is essential for effective organizations. Yet what often hinders initial progress for organizations in transformation is a limited understanding of a method for interaction that will facilitate learning. The following taxonomy can inform some methods for the process of collective learning.

Action learning, as a form of collective learning, uses the diverse perspectives of the group to understand and reflect on the issue of a single member. The intent is to help the presenter broaden his or her perspective concerning both the definition of the issue and possible solutions aimed at resolving the issue. It is the responsibility of the presenter to determine what actions will be taken. It is the responsibility of the group to help the presenter reflect on the actions he or she proposes to take.

In *dialogue,* the group is responsible for helping each member articulate his or her perspective on the issue at hand, including underlying assumptions, through questions and reflective listening. It is the responsibility of each member to ensure that his or her perspective has been articulated and is understood by the group. The group then listens for themes and begins to identify common ideas from each perspective. Those that are common are agreed on, and those that are not common are further considered to determine if they are essential to success (thus requiring some consensus on their acceptability) or can provide opportunities for local improvisation and innovation. In this case, the ideas are optional but nonetheless opportunities to learn from diverse approaches.

Team development, through both action and reflection, seeks to assist members of the team identify their personal contributions, which includes assumptions and responses to anxiety, that create and maintain the dynamics of the team. Once there is an understanding of how each person contributes to the dynamics, individuals are responsible to change themselves to create a healthier dynamic in line with the vision of the team.

The safety managers used an action-learning process in their meetings. Each meeting, individual participants presented what they were doing and then asked their team members to help solve any problems they may still be facing or to identify holes in their programs. It was critical that the action-learning process for this group required strong personal accountability. In the beginning, this prevented other members from trying to make everyone else do things like they did. A clear boundary was established that provided a level of comfort that nothing would be imposed. On the other hand, the personal responsibility also generated energy in the group. The process allowed for the pursuit of individual interests but did it in a collective manner. Ultimately, I believe this contributed to the high attendance and continued enthusiasm for the process.

Catalyst

The final piece of the infrastructure is a catalyst. It is too easy for groups to lose momentum. Learning-based change is a long-term process. In order to assist those pursuing change to maintain a sense of direction, it will be important to set goals that are consistent with the purpose of the organization. In addition, it is necessary for the group to have some information about how they are doing. Measures that indicate how much or how little progress has been made will act as external Disturbances and thus energize the learning process. The purpose of the catalyst is to continue to introduce new energy into the effort. There may be multiple catalysts. For instance, the nature of the action-learning process acts as a catalyst as it taps into the individual desire to improve oneself but protects self-determination as to how the improvement will take form.

The safety managers also included a more concrete learning mechanism that acted as a catalyst. They began each meeting by first populating their Learning Scorecard. The concept was simple: Each meeting started with asking those who took an idea away from the last meeting to identify the idea, who suggested it, what they did with the idea, and any resulting outcomes. The Learning Scorecard disciplined the group so that they kept track of their actions and then related their stories to others. It also provided a way for the group to evaluate the effectiveness of their learning meetings.

Observable Results

Regardless of how well a change initiative can be described or how sound a theory may seem, if there are no observable results, how successful can it be? According to Paul, Director of Health, Safety and Environmental Affairs, these observable results emerged from this effort:

- Increased comfort and trust among the managers
- Knowledge sharing even outside meetings
- The Learning Scorecard
- Managers replicating the effort with their own staffs

- Senior management asking for help and creating a similar type of effort among themselves
- A successful common management system
- Over $100,000 in savings from collaborative sharing

Leadership and Learning-Based Change

What is the connection between this story of successful organizational change and leadership? This story provides some valuable insight into the kind of leadership that allows profound organizational change to happen. All the pieces of a great plan can be in place, but whether the organization will have the courage and emotional stamina to let go of the past and achieve something new most often depends on its leadership.

> *Action learning, as a form of collective learning, uses the diverse perspectives of the group to understand and reflect on the issue of a single member.*

Generally, it is not that the leadership does the change work. To the contrary, the real improvements are achieved by the workers. However, leadership can either make or break the effort. If leaders create the right conditions and act in a manner consistent with the new vision that is growing, the capacity of the organization to change is expanded. But if leaders isolate themselves from the organization and continue to act in ways that are inconsistent with the desired future, they amplify the anxiety in the organization. Workers will be stifled and disillusioned. Energy will dissipate and the effort will not succeed. Unfortunately, the workers are often blamed for their lack of commitment while the leadership remains blind to its contribution to the failed effort.

The Safety/Loss Control change initiative was fortunate to have a leader, who was capable of learning and helping others learn. He demonstrated great maturity in his capacity to remain patient while committed to changing himself, rather than focusing on changing others. But, he was not alone in the effort. The members of the audit department showed their own courage by not requiring a traditional answer to the issue they had raised.

On page 101, Figure 8.3 shows the timeline of the learning-based change effort for this group. Appendix C at the back of this book includes an interview with the leader, Paul, who talks in depth about his experience of leading this effort.

Conclusion

In a learning-based change effort, the place change originates is within the individuals who are participating. When this happens, many of the fears and discomfort associated with change are discarded in favor of real dialogue. Leading such an effort takes a great deal of patience and self-regulation. However, in the end, the members grow in maturity and the organization increases its capacity to change again in the future.

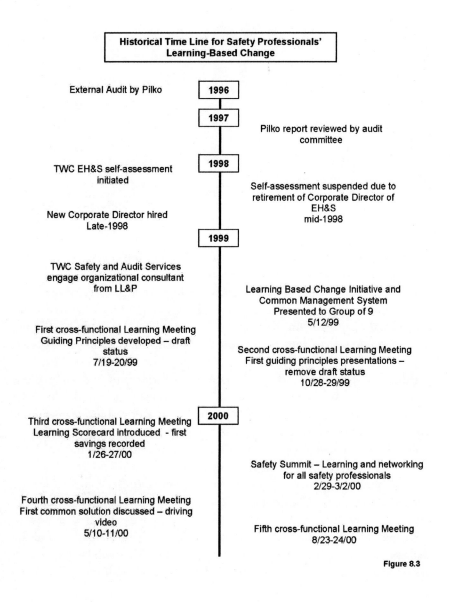

Historical Time Line for Safety Professionals' Learning-Based Change

External Audit by Pilko — **1996**

1997 — Pilko report reviewed by audit committee

TWC EH&S self-assessment initiated — **1998**

Self-assessment suspended due to retirement of Corporate Director of EH&S
mid-1998

New Corporate Director hired
Late-1998

1999

TWC Safety and Audit Services engage organizational consultant from LL&P

Learning Based Change Initiative and Common Management System Presented to Group of 9
5/12/99

First cross-functional Learning Meeting Guiding Principles developed – draft status
7/19-20/99

Second cross-functional Learning Meeting First guiding principles presentations – remove draft status
10/28-29/99

2000

Third cross-functional Learning Meeting Learning Scorecard introduced - first savings recorded
1/26-27/00

Safety Summit – Learning and networking for all safety professionals
2/29-3/2/00

Fourth cross-functional Learning Meeting First common solution discussed – driving video
5/10-11/00

Fifth cross-functional Learning Meeting
8/23-24/00

Figure 8.3

101

Chapter 9 - Conclusion

To emphasize the real benefit of this approach to leadership, the question that should always make its way to the forefront is this, "How does differentiated leadership lead to progress?" Times are such that organizations can no longer survive with leaders focused on telling others what to do and the rest of the organization allowing themselves to be taken care of by a leader. If progress is to be had, something more fundamental must change. Too much time, money and energy is going into "managing" the consequences of a failed paradigm. A paradigm of fear, immaturity, mistrust and self-centeredness cripple organizations. The real problems of the day are sequestered behind the unending political skirmishes in out of the way places within organizations. Truly visionary responses cannot be had because leaders fear the masses cannot handle the truth. Consequently, most leaders assume that those they lead will never pursue anything other than self-interest.

Differentiated leadership no longer places its faith in holding together this failed paradigm. Differentiated leaders recognize that they must begin the path of change by addressing their own anxiety and find a way to overcome their fear. Their depth of learning, both about themselves and the challenges surrounding them, must grow. As it does, they will be able to step out in courage and offer both the truth about current conditions and ask the questions which will allow a new vision to emerge. These new visions will take hold unlike those of the past, because they will come with a commitment to something greater than ones own comfort. They will endure because the new visions will not be the possession of a leader which must be sold to constituency in order to obtain compliance. Differentiated leaders realize that they must not only overcome their own fear, but must also tutor those around them in overcoming theirs as well. As leaders develop in their competency of defining themselves, they pass on this ability to all those who will listen. Such leaders not only lead change but they grow the maturity of the organization in the process. Differentiation results in identities of both worker and the organization being defined from within rather than imposed from outside. This strength of character enables organizations to take on the real root issues that have always seemed out of reach in the past. The energy of the people is directed in solving problems that count rather than managing the symptoms of an anxious and immature workplace.

There is a noble purpose for leadership still. It will not be welcomed with accolades in the beginning. It rocks the status quo to its foundation. Yet in the end, the great potential entrusted with human beings by their Creator finds its release in creating a world that works for all.

Epilogue

The last word in this book is a look back. If we are to have any hope of discovering a new tomorrow we must know something of our past. This chapter represents a type of reflection that might have some hope of changing the mindset of contemporary society. Human history is made up of times of progress and times of regression. By looking deeper at those periods, we may discover underlying structures of a mindset and worldview that can provide the understanding for promoting health and well-being for generations to come.

Times of Progress and Times of Regression

Before us is an entire history of people who have changed the world. Or have they? How much progress has been made? How much of what we live today is just a different version of what existed in the past? More important, can we conceive of a new tomorrow unless we understand the past and begin to ask some different questions about it? This Epilogue is the result of my attempt to understand from where we have come. The following chapter is a broad historical sketch that explores periods of progress and periods of regression in Western civilization from Rome until now. Perhaps understanding the past can provide insight as to the important conditions that sustainable change requires.

I will begin with a warning: Any solution to the set of complex problems leaders face in today's world will, in all likelihood, contain a *seed* that will ultimately reproduce the underlying causes of past failures. To be more precise, that *seed* is an attitude, a mindset, and a way of seeing the world that grows out of humanity's basic sense of mistrust and the corresponding need for control. This is more likely when solutions are seen as decisions, events, technologies, or answers. The *seed* is clever, lying dormant beneath the surface of any change. It has been concealed in revolutions, reformations, transformations, and new discoveries. With this in mind, let's begin by trying to create awareness of the nature of the *seed* and the kind of mindset that is necessary to manage it. It is such a subtle characteristic of humanity that I do not believe we will ever eradicate it from society. I do think, however, that with awareness and a diligent process for renewal, leaders can limit the damage the *seed* may cause.

It has been popular to cite the theories of Newton and Descartes as the genesis of our trouble.[1] Their work led to thinking that the world was a machine to control, rather than a living system. They did, indeed, play their part in creating our current society. Even so, if we have any hope of finding alternatives, we must take a broader look at our history. Imagine waking up some morning in the fourth century to realize that all the glue that had held civilization together (i.e., the Roman Empire) had come apart. The void this created did not last long. Feudalism rose to replace the missing government and give order back to the world—at least the human part. This system worked for a while until the fascination with power totally engulfed enough lords so as to make the peasants revolt. What seems to have been missed is the notion that there is a whisper in the presence of power that says, "If there is to be order, someone must tell and others must be told." "Throughout history, organization has been associated with processes of social domination where individuals find ways of imposing their will on others."[2] It is not difficult to see this sentiment in the beginnings of feudalism:

> *The prevalent condition, after the collapse of the once glorious Roman Empire, was chaos. As invariably occurs in a society lacking the instruments of law and order, whoever had the biggest fist, had the biggest say. People we would today call gangsters soon established their turf and, in exchange for their "protection," those they protected became their "serfs." Feudalism comprised the social order until the surfacing of towns in the twelfth century. Interestingly enough, because the lords created a system that only worked for them, they gave impetus to that which would be their own demise.*[3]

By the time Charlemagne tried to reunite the Western Empire, the religious institution of the West got the idea that it should do the "telling" and everyone else should "be told".[4] Not far removed from the early days of political persecution, the Church sought security in becoming the authority and battled with the monarchies for this privileged spot. The government could wreak havoc with people's lives right now, on earth, but the Church could make trouble in the future, or life everlasting. So, for some time, the Church enjoyed control. Unfortunately, it became so engrossed in the "telling" business that it forgot its primary job, which was to help keep people connected to the stories that gave meaning and purpose to their lives.

But the church, both East and West, also went on to produce (however pervasive it may have been) an essentially closed society—for the simple reason that it was by now inseparable from an institutional order. . . . Christendom, as an amalgam of church and state, became almost synonymous with the civil order, and the mission of the church shrank to maintaining the parameters of a temporal and spatial phenomenon.[5]

The Church would be the unifying force in the West for centuries and give rise to the great synthesis of the Middle Ages, resulting in monasteries, cathedrals, and universities. However, it would also provide a great harvest of exclusionary and oppressive acts, such as the Inquisition, excommunication, and the Crusades. With the threat of heaven on its side, the Church would keep other would-be powers at bay until the sixteenth century, when its corruption would be identified by one of its own. In 1517, a monk named Martin Luther ignited a spark that would divide the Holy Roman Church forever. "Having been raised in the late medieval atmosphere of fear and guilt, and in fear of judgment by the punishing severity of God, he found that the transactions which the church . . . offered him for the removal of those fears simply did nothing for him."[6] After a study of the book of Romans, Luther was sufficiently assured that the message of Christianity was not at all consistent with the corrupted condition of the Church, and he made that sentiment public.

Thus, it was the spiritual struggle of one monk that ignited the Reformation, but that lone effort would not have been sufficient for the movement that would emerge. Something deeper had to be present. Like the feudal lords before them, the clergy of the Church had replicated a system that only worked for a few. Yet there was a "prevalence of both deep piety and poverty among the Church faithful, while at the same time an often irreligious but socially and economically privileged clergy".[7] Luther's actions resulted in years of religious strife and war that paralleled the rise of the nation states. In the midst of the chaos created by the declining system, a void for order emerged and a new voice of order and power was born. "It was against the backdrop of massive cultural decay, violence and death that the 'rebirth' of the Renaissance took place."[8] The awakening of this cultural renewal was the Scientific Revolution.

When combined with human arrogance, the unrelenting force of power cut itself off from a source of meaning beyond humanity. In a series of works that continued to react to a millennium of abuse and oppression by the Church, the thinkers who would form the modern mindset turned to that which they could control: reason. "For when the titanic battle of the religions failed to resolve itself, with no monolithic structure of belief any longer holding sway over civilization, science suddenly stood forth as mankind's liberation."[9] As people's confidence in the human capability to control not only each other but also the universe increased, their separation from a transcendent Creator grew. Like an enthusiastic teenager with a driver's license and a minimum-wage job, who believes they have the world by the tail, the emerging modern mindset discarded traditional beliefs—in this case, ancient superstitions about how the world worked.

And so empiricism provided another foundation for science to become the "teller." If one could know how things worked and thus seemingly control them, he or she could tell others what to do. At the very least, a knowledgeable person would be validated and thus safe in a world unconnected from the cosmic spirit. Beginning with Scholasticism in the Middle Ages and continuing with the Scientific Revolution, the ability to explain things became an ever-important means of having power. The Renaissance and the Enlightenment came about as the Church experienced the Reformation.

> **Any solution to the set of complex problems leaders face in today's world will, in all likelihood, contain a seed that will ultimately reproduce the underlying causes of past failures.**

Like many movements, the Renaissance stemmed from noble intentions. Those who contributed to this cultural revolution sought to bring balance once again to human thinking. The Renaissance recovered the paradoxical thinking of the classical Greeks.[10] Nonetheless, it also contained the *seed*. Formed in mistrust and nurtured by a demand for certainty, the *seed* fully manifested itself as the modern mind left behind all of the wisdom hidden among the primitive, superstitious, childish, and oppressive beliefs of the Middle Ages.

The Scientific Revolution and its technological advances released humanity from dependence on the natural rhythms. Humankind became its own guide. Unencumbered by cosmological purpose, science was free to forge a reactive path toward reason and thus repeat that which caused darkness to fall on medieval Europe.[11] Science only recognized one end of a fundamental polarity. "The world revealed by modern science has been a world devoid of spiritual purpose, opaque, ruled by chance and necessity, without intrinsic meaning."[12] And while the illusion became much stronger as humanity learned to dominate nature, a greater sense of meaninglessness was ushered forth, culminating in the nihilism of Nietzsche.[13] This time, the danger of darkness would be greater, for humanity could now interrupt the movement of evolution itself.[14]

Although the modern scientific mindset was still the most powerful influence on most societal institutions in the beginnings of the New World, the other members of the ruling class—namely, religion and government—did not give up their struggle easily. "Where [the reformers] recognized medieval abuse, they righted it; but where they didn't, they perpetuated it."[15] Once again, leaders were drawn by the lure of power—the notion that someone must do the "telling" and others must "be told."

The Church never realized this. Thus, the American experiment began with the Puritans coming to the New World and seeking a new place to live. A century after they arrived, a Great Awakening occurred, whereby the Church in the United States found another opportunity to do the "telling." This religious movement was essentially about conformity, along with a prescription for morality. It is unfortunate that for most of the history of Christianity, the leaders have chosen to interpret the inclusive words of Jesus as a license to demand adherence to Scriptural codes at all costs. Moreover, whereas Jesus was concerned with changing people's hearts and minds, the Church mostly focused on compliant behavior. The intentions of Church leaders may have been good, but the truth is that they replicated the same attitude of dominance that had plagued all other institutions in Western society. This attitude reached a pinnacle with the Great Awakening in the sermons of Jonathan Edwards. His sermon "Sinners in the Hands of an Angry God" typifies the extent to which the religious system at the founding of the United States was based on fear:

> *The bow of God's wrath is bent, and the arrow made ready on the string, and justice bends the arrow at your heart, and strains the bow, and it is nothing but the mere pleasure of God, and that of an angry God, without any promise or obligation at all, that keeps the arrow one moment from being made drunk with your blood. Thus all you that never passed under a great change of heart, by the mighty power of the Spirit of God upon your souls; all you that were never born again, and made new creatures, and raised from being dead in sin, to a state of new, and before altogether unexperienced light and life, are in the hands of an angry God.*

Government remained a mainstay in the power-and-control game. The United States experienced a momentary reprieve after winning its revolutionary freedom from England. In a time of lucidity, the Founding Fathers created a system that would offer some buffer to the consolidation of power in the hands of the few. However, the current version of Jefferson's vision is pushing the system to the limit.

The twentieth century opened with a world war. Europe was left in devastation, thus leaving the door open for new dictators to emerge. From France to Russia, the countries of Europe were transformed into dictatorships.[16] Spurred on by economic chaos and the perceived threat of the advancing imperialism of Western market capitalism, Europe ended the second decade of that century divided by the growing power of Soviet communism.[17] Forged from the idealism of Marx, Communism was more than adequate to sustain the *seed* in the twentieth century. It could not do otherwise.

Marx was reactive to the oppression of the Western church as well as those who ascended to power and wealth through market capitalism. Again, like most revolutionaries, Marx saw a clear flaw in the dominant power of the day. However, in his passion to overthrow injustice, he propagated the fundamental ideology against which he was reacting.[18] "Karl Marx recognized that workers without choice are workers in chains. But his idea of breaking chains was for us to depose the pharaohs and then build the pyramids for ourselves."[19] Marx passed on the spirit of domination, providing a language for the government to subdue the commoner.

This same government did whatever was necessary to maintain stability. Order was maintained through forced compliance. Thus, Communism contained all the characteristics of the previous oppressive institutions. Soviet communists were reactive to a chaotic age and the perceived threat of a previous dominant institution. They were convinced that there was only one way to live: the Soviet way. This thinking was dominated by either/or logic.

Increasingly, the Soviet empire proved ineffective. When the system completely benefited the few, the many again spoke up in opposition. The Solidarity movement in Poland began the revolution that was the downfall of the Eastern bloc.

Here was an authentic workers' rebellion trying to hold the avowedly working-class government to its promises of the socialist dream, including self-rule by the people and less work for more pay. The demands and phenomenal growth of Solidarity spelled the bankruptcy of a regime which had outrageously mismanaged the country.[20] Any system that works for only a few is innately unsustainable.

As the market economy began to emerge, business began to develop in the Industrial Age. Like other institutions before it, business took on the notion that to create order; someone must "tell" and others must "be told." One of the greatest disciples of this new corporate order was Fredrick Taylor, who published The Principles of Scientific Management in 1911. Armed with the new tool of science and the belief that the world was a giant machine that could be controlled, Taylor believed that management could create precision output by controlling its employees. In his new corporate order, managers—with input from employees—would find the perfect form for each job through diligent scientific observation. Although Taylor did not totally dismiss the worker, his ideas grew out of control when employed in the real world: the hierarchy of market business. "Taylor was also somewhat disingenuous when he talked about 'the joint effort of the workers and the management,' since all his descriptions of the implementation of scientific management involve managers and engineers watching, timing and overseeing workers."[21] In Taylor's system, workers never really had any input. In addition, since management controlled all the capital, workers never saw the bonuses that were to have come with increased productivity.

Organizations still struggle with overcoming the influence of Taylor. Why? His ideas bred the illusion that a few at the top could control and predict worker output using the right combination of science and dominance. As far back as 1927, Mary Parker Follet's participatory management approach began calling for the fair and equal participation of all employees but was unsuccessful at curbing the influence of Taylor's scientific management.

The market economy was brought to a halt with the stock market crash in 1929, an infamous example of the wealth of the system being controlled by too few. "The reason [for the Great Depression] was the usual one, an irrational and self-destructive distribution of income that left the great mass of people, whether rural or urban, without the ability to buy what was being produced."[22] When the system worked for only a few, a revolt was in order. In fact, riots, rebellions, and some orderly political upheavals arose. This course of action in the marketplace set the stage for World War II.

The essential elements for a system of order based on fear and dominance are contained in the *seed*. Some theorists believe this basis of thinking has gained power for 10,000 years, during which time hunters and gatherers gave up their spears and baskets and traded them for plows.[23] Quinn describes the *seed* as the belief that there is "one right way to live."[24] Regardless of when it began, Western history shows that anytime there is chaos to be brought in order—with control being synonymous with order and the dominance of either/or thinking—the balance of power reverts to a few and a revolution eventually occurs. This is the natural rhythm of birth/death/rebirth.

In a time of lucidity, the Founding Fathers created a system that would offer some buffer to the consolidation of power in the hands of the few.

The great sadness is that each movement in history began to deliver the many from the oppression of the few yet ultimately contained the same fundamental essence. The dominating force changed, but the *seed* of dominance remained. Even those who seek control with the best of intentions may eventually be corrupted because using power to control others soon transforms the hero/rescuer into the tyrant. Why is this so? Power to control calls on that underlying fear and mistrust. And mistrust so unsettles us that even an illusion of certainty and control is better than trying to maintain mutual freedom.

The nature of the *seed* is as old as the tales of humanity. It can be found in the stories of creation. A basic human trait is always the incubating womb of nonsustainable institutions. In every person's heart of hearts, there is the tendency to mistrust. Throughout history, we have mistrusted each other along with God, nature, and the universe. That is why it has been so important to control and subdue all of people, God, nature, and the universe through science, philosophy, government, education, and religion. At the heart of our dark side may be the fundamental fear that we are not important enough. As society emerged from the Dark Ages, the Church was revealed as corrupt. Perhaps the combination of disillusionment with the Church and the rejuvenated confidence that came with the Renaissance set Western society on a course to distance themselves from God.

It is ironic that the solution to believing in a God that could not be completely understood and thus not trusted was to deny the very existence of God. Doing so has allowed us to create the world on our own terms. What are those terms? Namely, we live in a cold, impersonal universe in which everything, including humanity, is an accident and the sole purpose of existence is to survive. The fact is that modern Western society has been formed by a series of reactive measures. Even though each revolution, reformation, or transition was initiated by noble intentions, rarely was the fear associated with the past properly understood to the extent that the resulting trends could synthesize the "good ideas gone bad" with the centering ideas of the new age. Instead, the tendency toward mistrust continued to make the pendulum swing in the opposite direction. What still has not been recognized is that an extreme move in the opposite direction will be no more sustainable than the status quo.

The essence of the *seed* is maintained by the acceptance of illusion. I say illusion because the critical modes of thinking that support the *seed* contain half-truths that always promise what will never be delivered. Consider that the occurrence of either/or thinking, reactive certainty, security in exclusivity, or power used for unilateral benefit means that healthy, freedom-based systems will soon be gone.

Either/Or Thinking

It may be that how organizations think points them toward either sustainability or eventual collapse. One characteristic of the thinking in all the examples given thus far is the limited ability to hold onto the paradoxical nature of the universe. When organizations or societies look at the world in either/or terms, they undoubtedly look for simplistic answers to the dynamic issues of human civilization. This thought process sets the stage for seeing the world as a zero-sum game, in which security is obtained and sustained by excluding those that do not meet the standards of the establishment. Doing so creates the conditions wherein the good of the past is washed away in the flood of reaction to what is thereby creating a dynamic of reactive certainty. Ultimately, believing there is only one side to the coin limits any possibility of achieving the creativity, innovation, or freedom necessary to produce a sustainable organization.

Reactive Certainty

Why is it that although nearly every revolution begins as a noble resistance to an oppressive establishment, it soon becomes the target of the next revolution? As formerly mentioned, the groundwork is laid in the way individuals and organizations think about problems. When thought is grounded in simplistic, either/or terms, the only option in resisting a dysfunctional system is the opposite of that system. Rooted in a lack of historical perspective, the fear of the current power hurls the pendulum in the opposite direction.

Consider these examples: The Roman culture was devoid of meaning, so faith was the only solution. The Church was oppressive and myopic, so reason and science became a welcomed substitute.

> *The essence of the seed is maintained by the acceptance of illusion.*

Western civilization lamented in centuries of darkness because many refused to believe that an organization that had been proven corrupt might, in fact, have a kernel of truth hidden beneath the surface.

Just like the individual who deals with anxiety by acting without thinking, an organization or society will dash toward a new future without considering that the impetus for the old order also seemed to be a good idea—at the time. Blinded by fear, the organization or society moves to the extreme end of the continuum. But again, there is no sustainable life at the extremes.

Security in Exclusivity

Limited in vision and blinded by fear, the new order seeks security by limiting entrance only to those whom they say should belong. When security is sought in excluding others, the system will only work for the few. History is replete with examples, including the Jews of Nazi Germany, the blacks of apartheid South Africa, and even laborers who work in obscurity (since only management can see the whole picture). It may be that when limited vision is empowered by reactive fear, exclusivity is the only possible outcome. When it is believed that order can only exist through the dominance of those with power, progress will be curtailed. These three conditions seem always to be present in the downward spiral that gives rise to the next manifestation of the *seed*.

In addition to serving as gatekeeper—determining who is in and who is out—exclusivity takes root in the idea that "I am separate from you".[25] Being separate means that "I can act on you in any way I choose, and it will have no effect on me." Exclusivity is maintained by a series of illusions that are accepted to form a consensual lie. "We live in a society that perpetuates a great lie: that our social institutions, our communities, our lifestyles, our relationships with the environment, our shared worldview are basically okay, even desirable. . . . Everyone wants to be like us, which is good."[26]

Although these words describe our contemporary condition, the logic underlying them has supported many oppressive systems. That logic institutionalizes denial, and the type of system it supports always excludes its members from the problems. There is always a "them out there" to be blamed. In some sense, a false enemy creates an illusionary cohesion that provides a perverse kind of order for those who do not know how to live for the greater good.

Power for Unilateral Benefit

It is unclear whether the elements previously described create the conditions in which power is used unilaterally to benefit the few or result from that abuse of power. What does seem to be true is that when there has been a critical mass of this type of limited thinking—especially among those who have held positions of leadership—the result has been organizations and institutions based on fear, rather than freedom. When leaders find their security and validation in power, they ultimately require all in their charge to live with their demons.

Conditions of Hope

As important as it is to identify the problems that have continued to undermine human organizations throughout history, it is not enough. Again, this question is preeminent: How can people create organizations that are based on freedom rather than fear?

The answer cannot be found solely by identifying what inhibits a free and sustainable system. The catalytic thoughts that will lead to a more healthy system must also be identified. In fact, there have been some very encouraging periods of history, in which human creativity and contribution abounded. And even in the dark periods, certain conditions sometimes emerged and brought forth creativity and freedom. Those conditions can be described as synthesis thinking, transcendent meaning, and an adventurous spirit that made connection with others more available to all.

Synthesis Thinking

During the highpoints of the last two thousand years of history, a profoundly different way of thinking seemed to be present. Instead of believing in limited, either/or propositions, many were able to recognize that a lot of truths appeared to be mutually exclusive. Holding the various paradoxical realities in tension allowed a creative energy to emerge that moved people toward a more profound understanding of things.

Sense of the Transcendent

Another characteristic that was evident in these periods of revival was the keen awareness of and belief in something beyond humanity that gave purpose, meaning, and order to the universe. What is the importance of this? Isn't it just a manifestation of the superstitious thinking of primitive people who could not explain natural phenomena?

When organizations or societies look at the world in either/or terms, they undoubtedly look for simplistic answers to the dynamic issues of human civilization.

I suggest that it was important because those people had a greater sense of purpose and responsibility for the world they sought to understand. Unlike much of the pursuit of discovery for self-interest, the explorers of old pursued noble purposes. They sought to discover truth for the benefit of all and in service to the Creator. This should not be seen as something possessed only by a few. The conclusion is that human life and its settings are mysteries; and the emotional reaction is a feeling of humility and awe. We recognize that a human being is not master of the situation in which each of us finds himself as a consequence of having been called to life by forces whose nature and working he cannot fathom. The recognition of this impels a human being to make contact with these mysterious forces that hold him in His power. Man's motive in seeking to make contact with these trans-human forces is a wish to live, as much as possible, in harmony with them, and he desires this because he recognizes that the last word about Man and his destiny lies, not with Man himself, but with the Creator. This impulse seems to be common to all human beings, and all the historic religions are attempts to express it and to satisfy it.

The only thing that created this element in the best of human times was that individuals—especially individuals who ended up having a great influence on society—not only recognized this but also purposefully pursued it.

An Adventurous Spirit

In times in which human societies have taken great strides forward or have sought to return a needed balance to life, there have been individuals who have acted with courage. In some cases, these individuals set out on imaginative journeys to discover more of the world, as in the case of Columbus and Magellan, whose travels preceded the Renaissance. At other times, the adventurous spirit was contained in lives that sought to ask the important questions of life, often with great risk to themselves.

Not only did these adventurers ask important questions, but the risk they encountered was in the answers that challenged the status quo. For instance, Socrates was executed after being accused of corrupting young minds and introducing new gods. Jesus was crucified because his message was an enigma to both religious and secular politicians of his day. Galileo risked excommunication and death for suggesting that the earth was not the center of the universe. Likewise, Luther risked his life and vocation by questioning the foundation of the medieval Church, thus beginning the Reformation.

Many more examples of heroic leaders could be found in those brief moments in history in which the potential of human civilization was manifested. What is true of all of those individuals is that they did not let fear and comfort restrict their pursuit of truth and progress. They acted with great hope, which dissipated the societal anxiety that allowed creative innovation and expression to emerge.

An Appreciative Inquiry of History

Most of history has been spent on the extremes of some of life's most fundamental paradoxes. The Middle Ages, for example, was squarely focused on the pursuit of things spiritual. The Enlightenment moved to the other end of the spectrum by pursuing things rational and scientific with singular purpose. Before and after these eras were civilizations that held the dual nature of reality in tension. The result of this courageous effort not to settle for the simplistic gives us a potential map for discovering an improved society. This map can be found in the words of the Ancient Greeks, of Jesus of Nazareth, and of those thinkers that preceded the Renaissance.

Ancient Greeks

What was different about the Ancient Greek civilization that set it apart in Western history? The Greeks were driven by a determined pursuit of clarity and system. The search for the Beautiful, the True, and the Good led them to a profound way of thinking:

The constant interplay of these two partly complementary and partly antithetical sets of principles established a profound inner tension within the Greek inheritance, which provided the Western mind with the intellectual basis, at once unstable and highly creative, for what was to become an extremely dynamic evolution lasting over two and a half millennia.[27]

The richness and strength of the Greek worldview proved capable of enduring the fall of Greece to Rome. Roman conquerors held onto the Greek culture and hastened the spread of that culture during the Pax Romana, when travel was expanded as a result of having achieved order in the political realm and making advances such as roads. This set of circumstances set the stage for what arguably has been the single most influential movement in Western history: Christianity.

Christianity

By the time Jesus was born in the small town of Bethlehem in Ancient Israel, the Roman world was in great need of assistance in recovering a sense of meaning. "In the course of the unsettled Hellenistic era, something like a spiritual crisis appears to have arisen in the culture, its members impelled by the newly conscious needs for personal significance in the cosmos and personal knowledge of life's meaning."[28] The Greek philosophers and the practical Roman thinkers had set the stage for the most profound revelation in history.

Regardless of your religious views, the message of Jesus contained all the elements necessary to counter the *seed.* Inherent in the Gospel was clearly a worldview that recognized the mystery in the paradoxical nature of the universe. "The last shall be first and the first shall be last." To find your life, you must lose it. Life will come out of death. In addition, there was a proclamation of inclusivity such as the world had never considered before. The God of love would conquer all divisions:

> *In times in which human societies have taken great strides forward or have sought to return a needed balance to life, there have been individuals who have acted with courage.*

In contrast to the Hellenic focus on great heroes or beauty or social status, Christianity universalized salvation, asserting its availability to slaves as well as kings, to simple souls as well as profound thinkers, to the ugly as

117

well as the beautiful, to the sick and the suffering as well as the strong and the fortunate. . . . In Christ, all divisions of humanity were overcome.[29]

It would prove unfortunate that the followers of Jesus never quite had the capacity to embody this ideal in the world, like he did. Nevertheless, the necessary components for a metanoia of society were delivered by this young Rabbi:

The "repentance" Jesus called for was not so much a prerequisite as it was a consequence of the experience of the dawning Kingdom of God. It was less a backward-moving and paralyzing regret for past sinfulness than a progressive embrace of the new order, which made ones old life appear inauthentic and misdirected by comparison.[30]

Jesus revealed the mystery of the paradoxical universe; he transcended the limited belief in a zero-sum game and reconnected humanity to transcendent meaning. The fundamental dualistic split of the universe, matter and spirit, would be mended in the incarnation of the Logos. And while the spirit of the message would soon be lost for nearly one thousand years, it would be recovered by a lowly monk in the twelfth century. This recovery set the stage for the Renaissance.

The Renaissance

Stability, prosperity, and relative peace renewed the interest in learning and, in particular, the philosophy of the Classical era. Emerging out of ten centuries of darkness, Thomas Aquinas recovered the synthesis thinking of old. "Influenced by Aristotle's teleological concept of nature's relation to the highest Form and the Neoplatonic understanding of the all-pervasive One, Aquinas declared a new basis for the dignity and potential of man."[31] Aquinas's remarkable ability to reunite the divided faith and reason—human and divine, nature and spirit—set the stage for the emergence of the Renaissance.

Spurred by the adventurous spirit of men such as Columbus, the mind of a society that had been locked up for centuries by fear and either/or thinking emerged to enjoy great creativity.[32] Within a fifty-year span, the world would be proven to be round, not flat; the sun would be found to be the center of the solar system, not the earth; and the first steps would be taken toward reforming the medieval church. The renewed curiosity and synthesis thinking allowed an inclusive spirit to resurface momentarily as the many contradictory notions of life were considered side by side. The church would be recovered for the parishioners and not be just the domain of the clergy, and the printing press would be invented, revolutionizing the ability to proliferate diverse thoughts in the form of printed texts. Although the West would head straightaway into a myopic reaction to the past, which would result in the modern mindset and all its limitations, the emergence from the Dark Ages brought, once again, the presence of paradoxical thinking, courageous inclusivity, and a reconnection with transcendent meaning.

Conclusion

I cannot say how the needs for power, certainty, and exclusive privilege have interacted throughout time. This Epilogue has dealt only with very broad brushstrokes of history. In the midst of the many eras highlighted are many incidents that would contradict the primary idea that I propose. Nonetheless, it can be said that when power becomes tainted in the name of exclusivity, it facilitates the dominance of fear. Conversely, when power is used to include, to multiply itself, instead of being seen as a limited resource, it can inspire a level of creativity only possible in freedom.

For leadership not to fall prey to the corruption of power, leaders must think paradoxically. The courage to do so will come out of the conviction of unconditional value that is the gift given to every creature by the Creator. The belief in your unconditional value facilitates the willingness to accept limitations and explore them, rather than hide and ignore them. Like kings of old, leaders must find "fools" who will reflect reality back at them.[33] If leaders want to be effective, they must refrain from trying to control others and must give constant vigilance to managing themselves as they attempt to see the world more clearly.

Appendix A - Assessing Your Differentiated Response

The more differentiated a leader becomes the greater their capacity for trust and collaboration. This increased capacity means they have less of a need for control and certainty. The following assessment provides some questions to help you begin thinking about the quality of your interaction with others. The goal of this assessment is to give you a starting point and then to watch for improvement. It is a life-long journey to become a more effective, differentiated leader. Use these questions as a way to increase the perspective on your abilities and highlight areas for learning.

The Collaborative Leader Assessment

By Greg Robinson, Ph. D.

Introduction:

The more differentiated a leader becomes the greater their capacity for trust and collaboration. This increased capacity means they have less of a need for control and certainty.

The following assessment provides some questions to start thinking about the quality of your interactions with others. The goal of this assessment is to provide a starting point and then to watch for improvement. It is a life-long journey to become a more effective, differentiated leader.

Use these questions as a way to increase the perspective on your abilities and highlight areas for improvement.

Instructions:

Use the scale on the continuum after each question to rate the person's abilities. The scale runs from 1 to 7 with descriptions under each end of the continuum. Please use the entire scale to reflect your most accurate response and be as honest as possible.

The name you put on the assessment is the person for whom you are giving the feedback.

Your name will not be attached to your comments, just your position which will be labeled with other similar position responses.

While it is important to be thoughtful, don't agonize over each response. This assessment should not take more than 15 minutes. Please add your comments in the section after each question to explain the number you chose. This explanation will help provide context for the person in order for them to improve.

Feedback Tips:

Be Behavior Specific - Give details about what specifically was done well or what might be done differently. Focus on behaviors that can be changed, not personal characteristics or interpretations.

Be Brief and Concise - Too much feedback can be overwhelming and isn't absorbed well. It's often reasonable to select the most important point or two, and leave the rest for another opportunity.

Be Honest – It can be difficult to provide constructive feedback. It is important to remember that by not providing honest observations, we limit the ability of others to learn, grow and improve.

For a copy of this Collaborative Leader Assessment, go to

www.challengequest.com

The Collaborative Leader Assessment

Name of person you are rating: **Date:**   **Your Role:**

Write the number you choose in the Score box.

1. To what extent does he/she seek views different than his/her own views?

```
     1      2      3      4      5      6      7
```

Avoids or ignores
differences

Actively seeks out
different perspectives

Score: ☐

Comments:

2. To what extent does he/she build upon or explore differences that are raised?

```
     1      2      3      4      5      6      7
```

Quickly eliminates
differences

Actively explores the perspectives
and concerns of others

Score: ☐

Comments:

```
     1      2      3      4      5      6      7
```

Becomes defensive if others
question his/her ideas

Actively seeks to understand the
perspective of those who may
disagree with him/her

Score: ☐

Comments:

Total Score for Item #2: ☐

© Greg Robinson Ph.D.

3. When tension rises in a discussion, how does he/she respond? Do they seek a quick fix such as taking control and quashing the issue, withdraw, change the subject, use humor or give quick agreement to relieve the tension or do they acknowledge the tension and seek to understand the root issues behind it?

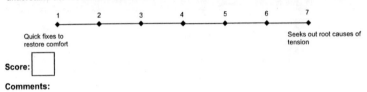

Quick fixes to
restore comfort

Seeks out root causes of
tension

Score:

Comments:

4. To what extent does he/she place a priority on the quality of interpersonal interactions?

Task focus only

Balance of task and
relationship focus

Score:

Comments:

© Greg Robinson Ph.D.

The Collaborative Leader Assessment

5. To what extent can he/she clearly and calmly articulate his/her own position on an issue?

| 1 | 2 | 3 | 4 | 5 | 6 | 7 |

Never reveals own
position

Always clearly articulates
own position

Score:

Comments:

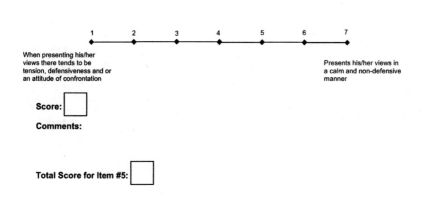

| 1 | 2 | 3 | 4 | 5 | 6 | 7 |

When presenting his/her
views there tends to be
tension, defensiveness and or
an attitude of confrontation

Presents his/her views in
a calm and non-defensive
manner

Score:

Comments:

Total Score for Item #5:

6. To what extent does he/she ask questions rather than give advice or answers?

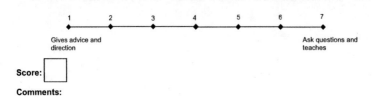

Gives advice and
direction

Ask questions and
teaches

Score:

Comments:

7. To what extent does he/she purposefully seek to learn from their experience and the experience of others?

Past experience is
never mentioned
unless it is to place
blame.

Past experience is
reflected upon in a
purposeful way.

Score:

Comments:

8. How transparent is his/her thinking process when forming views or making decisions?

Tends to speak in
absolute statements
and broad
generalizations

Clearly identifies
assumptions that inform
their opinion or decision

Score:

Comments:

© Greg Robinson Ph.D.

The Collaborative Leader Assessment

9. To what extent does he/she seek to have others assume responsibility for themselves, their actions and positions rather than blame?

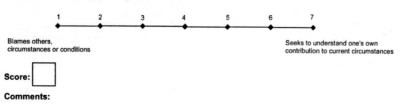

Blames others,
circumstances or conditions

Seeks to understand one's own
contribution to current circumstances

Score:

Comments:

10. How does he/she tend to understand problems?

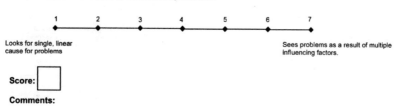

Looks for single, linear
cause for problems

Sees problems as a result of multiple
influencing factors.

Score:

Comments:

11. How well does he/she see the "bigger picture"?

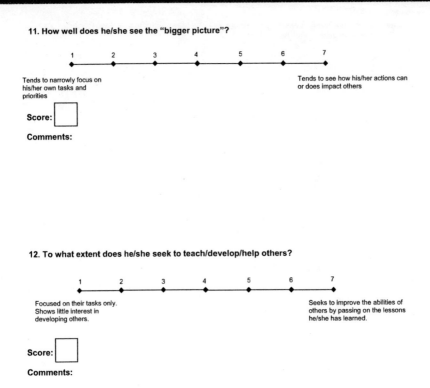

```
     1        2        3        4        5        6        7
```

Tends to narrowly focus on
his/her own tasks and
priorities

Tends to see how his/her actions can
or does impact others

Score:

Comments:

12. To what extent does he/she seek to teach/develop/help others?

```
     1        2        3        4        5        6        7
```

Focused on their tasks only.
Shows little interest in
developing others.

Seeks to improve the abilities of
others by passing on the lessons
he/she has learned.

Score:

Comments:

13. To what extent is he/she able and willing to delegate and empower others?

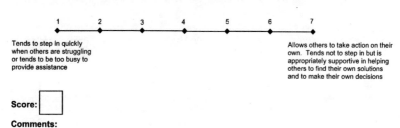

| 1 | 2 | 3 | 4 | 5 | 6 | 7 |

Tends to step in quickly
when others are struggling
or tends to be too busy to
provide assistance

Allows others to take action on their
own. Tends not to step in but is
appropriately supportive in helping
others to find their own solutions
and to make their own decisions

Score:

Comments:

14. From your perspective, what is this person's best qualities?

15. If you could make one recommendation on an area that this person could develop that would make them more effective, what would you recommend? What would the payoff be for such a change?

The Collaborative Leader Assessment

Results

The composite scores on this assessment form are plotted on the continuum of 3 core abilities: Emotional Maturity, Critical Reflection, and Systems Thinking. These are three essential competencies for effective collaboration.

Emotional Maturity – the ability to monitor the emotional state of self and others, to regulate oneself in the face of anxiety rather than be reactive and to tolerate high levels of emotional discomfort. (Use the score from items 1,2,3,5 and plot the average)

Critical Reflection – the willingness and ability to learn from experience, to uncover and challenge one's assumptions and the willingness to ask questions rather than simply provide advice. (Use the score from items 6,7,8 and plot the average)

Systems Thinking – the ability to see the interdependencies between things, to see the bigger picture, to seek root causes rather than symptoms and the ability to change self rather than others. (Use the score from items 9,10,11 and plot the average)

The fourth critical competency focuses on the leader's willingness and ability to not only get work accomplished but to also facilitate the development of others. Organizations that have well developed leaders at all levels are more capable of responding to a changing environment.

Facilitative Leadership - the ability and willingness to focus on interpersonal process and the task at the same time, the ability and willingness to teach others and the willingness and ability to allow others to learn from doing without the leader being too close or too far away. (Use the score from items 4,12,13 and plot the average)

130

Appendix B - Brent Coussen's Interview

Manager of Information Technology Consulting Company

Greg [Author]: Can you compare the culture of your group, the Consulting Company, now to how it was when it started?

Brent: We have gone through a couple of things. Number one, we started out pretty small so there wasn't a whole lot of culture there. And because it was a group that combined parts of two other groups—there wasn't a whole lot of anything there. Then on top of it, we tripled in size in nine months; that, in itself, means that you actually bring in lots of diversity from different people's standpoints. If we did have a culture, it was an individual culture. I think what we have been able to do is to create it. I think there is a lot of power in that – being able to ask, "Okay, how do we want to mold this? What do we even mean by *culture?*"

G: How would you describe the current culture?

B: I think it is a collaborative environment that people feel comfortable with. People have bought into our action-learning teams. The attitude is that "I can help shape this into what I want it to be." I think in a fairly short time, less than a year, that we have created an identity for ourselves. Culture and identity probably go hand in hand. It wasn't just one day it was this and the next day it was that. It really has evolved.

G: How would you compare your consulting company with the typical IT (Information Technology) department inside a large corporation?

B: Part of our structure and part of the culture is that we are really a small company inside a large corporation. We have perpetuated that with many of the things that we have done—meaning that we have given ourselves that identity. Because we are a consulting group, we have to react very quickly and stay on the leading edge of the technology curve. We own no work – meaning that all of our work is something that someone else is willing to pay us or give us to do.

G: How successful has your organization been to this point?

B: Very successful. Much more successful than I think any one person imagined it could be. Given that we started with eight or nine people in April 2000 with an original goal of being able to break even in any one of our first twelve months. We got into it and just exploded. In reality, by the end of the year, we had tripled in size. We had not only broken even but had actually made a slight profit—a profit that we gave back to the corporation. We actually were able to recover all of our costs, which is our charter and part of our bylaws. The organization had given us the nine months of 2000 to get our act together. But in reality, it just took off, and I think by July, we had already started recovering our costs each month. By the end of the year, we had not only recovered but made up all of the losses we had the first three months. I think that is the financial success. I think the other success really lies in the fact that we have an organization that people are wanting into. People are trying to position themselves through interviewing or job postings to get into our company. At first, there was a lot of apprehension of the people that were in it, wondering "Is this thing going to last? Can we sustain it? Is it a fluke?" We have none of those questions now. It is just the opposite: "How fast do we see it growing? What types of business practices and skill sets do we want to continue to take on within the organization?"

G: What do you think are some of the key things that have contributed to your being successful so quickly?

B: Number one: getting the right people in the group. That absolutely has to be there. With the right people, it is more of an attitude first, aptitude second, philosophy third. When I am trying to bring somebody in, that is the way I look at it. The second thing is that once you have somebody in the group, you must have the means for them to actually increase their attitude and aptitude—things like our action-learning teams. Also, the monthly group meetings that we have really help create the cohesiveness. We have even assigned one person that part of his day-to-day responsibilities is culture. He is our culture person. He has done a lot to help. Part of it is having fun. You try to ensure that we are able to have some fun along the way. Part of it is celebrating our success. We probably haven't done that as much as we could, but it is recognized. It is recognized not only by me but by other management people within our organization. So, it really is a combination of multiple things.

G: What is interesting is that none of those things really are brand-new ideas. They have been around for a long time. What do you think has helped you be successful?

B: They are not new ideas. The only thing that I would even consider a new idea in my mind was the action-learning teams. And that was really formalizing a concept. I think that is really what we have done; we have formalized some of this. Everybody knows that you want to have the right kind of culture in a group. But how many people actually assign somebody to say part of your responsibility is the culture, "King of Culture." We have been deliberate in some of those efforts. We have been deliberate in the sense of saying everybody wants training. All groups say that training is important, but we were deliberate. This was a group decision, not a management decision. As a group, we said we will go through three weeks a year of training. Now, what we are not deliberate with is telling somebody exactly what they are going to do with those three weeks of training. It is an individual choice of how you use those three weeks. But everyone will do it. I think that there is an element of "Yes, these are somewhat old ideas or things that we have all talked about in our careers." But there is, and it is a small little turn that I don't think there is anything difficult about – saying we will be deliberate in the way we do it. We will make some proclamations that these are a few core things that we are going to do. Once a month, we hold a group meeting, which is always the second Monday of the month. People put it on their schedule. It's a long lunch. Additionally, once a quarter, we have all-day group meetings—the second Monday at the beginning of each quarter. People just start thinking that way saying "Okay, here is who is in your group and then letting the group take it from there." Identifying a coach. We all want coaching, but we actually formalize it by saying "Okay, here is a person who can help you with your coaching areas. And by the way, they are available to do that. Not only available, but we are actually paying them to do that for us."

G: What has been most difficult?

B: For the group, it is just believing. When you have everything from a new college grad, who has all the energy and feels on top of the world and is excited about their career, clear to the 30-plus-year veteran of corporate America, who has seen virtually all of the cycles take place within their career, and you bring them together there are two senses. There is a sense of, "Wow, this is exciting. I am wide eyed, and I just want to take on everything". And then there is the other side of "I have seen these things come and go. What is going to sustain this one?" I think it has been hard combining these two senses. We are not completely there yet, but we are a lot closer than when we started.

For me personally, it has been just trying to understand that some of these things that we are talking about right here are important. Because on the other hand, we have got 40-plus projects going on, all with times frames and level of efforts, etc. How do we continue to keep the focus on culture? What I have had to realize is that it is my responsibility to do that. I have to continue to reinforce that these things are good. People believe that they are good. People want them. But they aren't necessarily willing to take ownership of them unless they think that they have got management or somebody there to allow it to happen. A good example with the group, as well as with any individual, is that we talked about training for three or four months. How we were going to do training. What we were going to do. In one of our group meetings, I finally said, "You know, we have X amount of budget this year for training, and we haven't spent hardly any of it. Why is that? We talked about it and said you can go do whatever you want to do." The group response was, "Well, we don't have time." So somebody asked, "What happens if we require it?" It changed the whole attitude of the group. All of a sudden, they now saw that we bought into it so much so that we said we were requiring it. Not only that, but it is a performance measure. If you don't do it, you will get "dinged." If you do it, that is good; you have met the requirement. That changed the whole attitude.

G: What has surprised you during this learning-change process?
B: What surprised me personally is that I have to constantly reinforce it. That has been an "ah-hah" for me. I think in the group, we would say that it has come together quicker than what we may have expected and that other people in the larger organization are looking around and noticing that it is different. They don't really know why. But you get, "This thing is different, what really is going on there?"

G: What mistakes have you made? What would you do differently?
B: That goes back to the reinforcing. When we got started, there was a lot of excitement around it. We did a few things up front to help combine these two partial groups into one. We immediately hired some other people. There was a level of excitement there for the first month or two. We had momentum on our side; things were rolling. We went through a period of two or three months where we weren't really paying attention to some of the culture stuff. We initiated it, we put it out there, but we weren't really measuring it in a nonquantitative way. All of a sudden, we lost the momentum and it started going back down the hill. What I would have done differently is to have

jumped on that quicker. It took an additional amount of energy to get it restarted. It didn't come to a complete halt, but I do think that people in their minds thought there was a lot of hype—that it was all good, but now we were going back to the same old stuff. We had to step in and say, "No, we are not doing the same old stuff. We really are trying to do some things differently." We did that with the positive reinforcement, group meetings, and setting a few rules in place. I think we have the momentum again. I actually think that this time, the momentum is very sustainable.

G: What unintended results have you seen from this?
B: One is that we have people lining up, wanting to get into the IT Consulting Company. That is a good consequence. It makes the hiring process much easier, and we are really able to be selective. Another good one, I think, is that as a whole, the group has become a lot stronger. We have these small teams that are just people collaborating. It doesn't take a whole lot to get that initiated. There is a lot of trust. In fact, I think that is somewhat intentional, but it is certainly not something that we could say: "We are going to be a trusting organization." But it has happened. I think that overall, they trust each other, the management team, and they have some trust in themselves. One of the negative results is trying to manage the growth. I can personally now see when I hear about small companies that cave in on their own success; that is something we have really had to fight. It takes a lot of energy. It is a good problem to have, but it definitely can be a problem.

G: What is it about the leadership of this group—which includes yourself, the director above you, and the board of directors from the Consulting Company—that has allowed this kind of stuff to emerge? Especially the trust.
B: Well, Chris [the director of Strategic Development and Brent's boss] is definitely the visionary. Chris had the vision on how this would work. I attribute a lot of the initial momentum to his insight. Doing some of the things, like calling ourselves a Consulting Company, which is a funny name for a company within a large corporation. Putting together a board of directors gave us an opportunity to get buy-in with some of our key clients because our board of directors really are the people that we go to get the work from. They are not only a board of directors, but they also help provide work for us. They have buy-in both ways. We literally have by-laws that we have drafted. We had initial ones, and we have added additional ones. We have changed some of the initial ones, but I don't think we have deleted any. Part of that base was really important. I think from an ongoing effort, once we got the base there, it really became that what people were asking was "Are they going to do what

they say they are going to do?" They were looking not only at me and Chris but at you [Greg], the CIO, and even the board. They wanted to know if we were really going to follow through with this. And I think we have. I think they are also looking for how transparent you are. When things are good, do you say they are good? When things are not good, do you say, "Hey, we need to do something here?" I feel we are a very transparent company. That didn't happen day one. In order for me to be transparent with the group, Chris has to be transparent with me. It takes multiple factions. I do believe I could be transparent to the rest of the group and not have upper-management support, but it would be much more difficult.

G: What are some of the major obstacles that you have faced?
B: Answering the questions of "What is this group? What are they doing?" You get the multiple facets that way of "Is this a prima donna group?" That is one we continue to hear. Quite frankly, when I first started, I was saying, "Thank you." Externally, we have to say, "No, we are here to provide a service." When people start making those kinds of statements, they are really saying that we sort of sit above the rest. But, I think we have to separate ourselves in some of our skills. The other obstacle, which I talked about earlier, is the quick growth. Initially, combining two diverse group parts, which were not even full groups but parts of two groups, and making them one team was an obstacle. [*Author's note:* These two groups came together after a downsizing, so morale was low going into this.]

G: What is the value of this kind of change to an organization?
B: I think it is immense. I think it is off the scale. We are talking about some things like a role-based organization, a truly role-based organization, where people, no matter where they are on the organizational chart or from a job-grade perspective, can play multiple roles. In fact, the only thing that keeps them from playing multiple roles is their own set of skills and desires. I think that is invaluable. I think some more value for the organization is that the organization is able to leverage us in the sense that we take on projects or tasks that they need done but don't have the current people or resources to do. So they can plug and play us in multiple ways and not have to staff up on their own. So we can respond more quickly, as a rule. On top of that, we have people in our group that can do multiple things. There is no such thing as being pigeonholed in this group. In fact, I cannot afford to have a person who only has one skill, because over time, that skill is going to change and then I won't know what to do with them. From a hiring perspective, that is one thing that I am always looking for: Do they want to take on other skills or roles? Parts of the corporation saw it right out of the chute. I think now,

even if we did a survey across the entire corporation, they would all say that one thing we can do is respond quickly and help them with their needs with the right kind of skilled people to meet those needs. If we weren't doing that, we wouldn't be growing. We would have reached a plateau. In fact, I still don't know when the curve is going to somewhat flatten out.

G: One of the things that you have been trying to create is a culture that promotes and supports continuous learning at both the individual and organizational levels. How would you define *learning*?

B: I can't define it in a sentence. I know that. I think learning is constantly looking for the next opportunity. Constantly evaluating what your opportunities are and then taking actions to get you in line with what those are going to be. Learning really is continuous. There is no such thing as learning as a noun all by itself or a verb just in a sentence. It really has to be continual. It has to be focused. I think that is something that people sometimes miss. You have to focus your learning to get to where you want to go. It has to be supported by the organization. An individual has to be willing to do some things on their own. I tell you, one thing I think we miss sometimes in the academic world is that you walk in as a high school student, sit down with a counselor, and they show you what your curriculum is going to be for the next four years. Then you go to college, and the first thing they do is hand you a syllabus and a curriculum. They say if you want to be a business major, here is what you take every semester for the next four years. You go to graduate school, and it is the same thing. I am thinking about my own background there. We make it structured in that sense, and it needs to be, but what I think we miss sometimes is that we have to really apply ourselves. What happens when you get into the business world is that it is very seldom that somebody sits down and hands you a syllabus and a career plan. We don't do that with people and their careers. We don't sit down and say, "Okay, this year do 1, 2, 3, 4 and the next year do 5, 6, 7, 8. By the time you are forty years old, you will be in this spot. By the time you are sixty, you can retire to the Gulf Coast of Florida." That may disillusion people. On the other hand, I think that if you do provide just a little bit of guidance and enforce that, then people will make the right decisions for themselves. They just need to know that you are going to support them.

G: What does a learning culture, such as this, require from you as the leader?

B: Well, my opinion has changed. I had to be the catalyst and provide the vision. I don't really like that statement—that I have to provide the vision— because it makes it sound like there is somebody already there. But it really does require that. *Vision* meaning we had to set up the action-learning teams. You [Greg] had to do the same with the coaching. I don't know what the next one is going to be. We had to do the same with the culture. So, it really does require somebody there to take a step of faith a little bit maybe, but really it is more of "Here is a way for you to reach the ends of your means." Then, on top of that is vision, in the sense that "If we can do this, we are going to be better." So it is a vision/leadership thing. I downplayed that for too long at the time. I thought that it would just sort of happen, but it doesn't. It takes a catalyst to make it happen.

G: Has your own personal approach to learning changed since you have been involved in this?
B: Oh, yeah. My approach has been more around leadership and what it takes to be an effective leader in a learning environment than what it is to be a participant. And I thought if you were just an advanced participant, people would follow along, but it really takes leadership. That is sort of a self-serving statement, but I have seen the things that I am now learning and the books that I am reading are all around leadership or organizational management.

G: Any other thoughts or ideas you have about this whole endeavor?
B: It takes a step of faith. You have to be able to go out and get on the end of the limb. You don't have to understand everything about how it is going to take place, meaning that you don't have to know from A to Z what the order might end up being. In fact, I don't think that you can anyway. Having somebody that knows more about it than you is really important. We have leveraged you [Greg] for this—learning who you can leverage. You have to build trust with people that way. I think one thing, and this goes back to the leadership, is finding who you can work with. We worked with you on the action-learning side of it and some on the coaching.

If we can establish key relationships, you just become so tight with what you are trying to do. It takes longer. There is no such thing as a microwave approach to it—for instance, us saying, "Hey, we are going to go to leadership and learning and get the consultant of the week." We could get people to do that, and we would get some value. But I really think over time, you get an exponential amount of value when you develop that relationship first. It continues on.

Appendix C - Paul Hunter's Interview

Director of Health, Safety and Environmental Affairs

Greg [Author]: For the sake of this conversation, *team* is referring to the group of cross-functional safety professionals that are a part of this initiative, not your team in corporate or the environmental group. Can you compare the relational atmosphere of the team now compared to when you first started this project?

Paul: There are at least three things that have changed. For starters, they know each other now, which was not the case before. They may have known the names of their counterparts before, but not much more. For example, Rick at this refinery knew John at that refinery, but they did not know the rest of their peers across the company. So if it has accomplished anything, it has at least got them to know the names of the other safety and loss-control practice leaders in the company. The second thing I have noticed is that they are starting to do a lot more cross-communication with each other outside our learning meetings. There are some that still have to come along in the process to understand, but the ones that really get it are not hesitating to just pick up the phone and call across company lines and use resources from other people. The last thing is the interaction in the learning meetings themselves. The team has opened up more because they understand the process and they understand how they are not under the gun or under fire—they are not putting on a show. They just need to tell it like it is and trust that everyone else tells it like it is for them, and then they work together to solve issues or borrow stuff from each other. In the first meetings, they were no where near doing anything like that.

G: What are some of the observable results you have noticed coming from this project?

P: Well, the Learning Scorecard is one for sure. That is the formalized tool in observing the results from the meetings. Another result, which I think is a big one, is that I am starting to see this type of an effort happen within the Energy safety professionals. How Energy Services has gone about building their best-practices organizations looks a lot like what we are doing here. And it is starting to happen not only with the safety professionals but with their senior leaders also. A third thing I've noticed is how the Safety Summit was a tangible result in the fact that these guys know each other and call each other. I think these results are all things that point to what this effort has accomplished.

G: What surprised you about this learning and change process?

P: Two things. That it would take such an effort on my part and the facilitator's part. And two, how difficult it is to grasp for some people. That for whatever reason, the concept is baffling until they have worked through it. That surprised me.

G: What has been most difficult?

P: Keeping the group on point and reiterating the purpose and how the learning works. Having to repeat that message over and over and over. Because again, it may be my personality is such that I get it and I don't understand why they don't get it. So, I think for me the difficult part is the surprise of going back again and saying, "Okay, for some reason we are not getting it. Let's just keep building upon this one step at a time."

G: Do you have any ideas on why you think it is so difficult for some people to grasp?

P: Part of it is their approach, part is their experiences in their professional careers, and the other part is their comfort zones. Another reason is probably their perception that their senior leader, whoever that is to them, doesn't support the effort or doesn't understand the effort.

G: In your opinion, what are some other major obstacles to this kind of an effort in an organization?

P: For one, the resource and time commitment without the perceived value up front is the initial obstacle. Now that we are using the Learning Scorecard and starting to look at the values that are coming out of it, it doesn't seem to be as much time away from my job as much as time to make my job more effective. So I think the first major hurdle is changing the attitude of "Here comes another meeting," "Here comes another flavor of the month," or "I don't have the time to do this." Then the subsequent obstacles are to keep it rolling and to keep showing the value—to start getting them to see where we have been, where we are now and the change that has taken place.

G: Are the other members of this learning team beginning to take any ownership in keeping it going on themselves?
P: Well, they look to me to coordinate it. But I think that some are taking responsibility by the fact that they are there at every meeting.

G: Have there been any unintended results or things that have come out of this that you didn't anticipate going in? Good or bad.
P: Yeah, the Energy group is starting to copy bits and pieces of this effort and use it. That could be good or bad. We don't know yet. We will wait and see. Another result that was a surprise was how much of an effort it is to keep the focus and to keep the purpose out there. It sounds easy: "Hey I got a meeting once every quarter I have to coordinate with these guys," and I sit back and let them do all the work. That is not exactly what happens. A third unintended result is that I am getting more calls and requests from various people than I thought I would. I wasn't fully prepared resource or time commitment wise to help with these other requests.

G: How do you make something that changed like this sustainable?
P: You have to find a process. You have to find goals and purposes for the process. You make it clear to the participants what their role is and what the value is for them and what is expected of them. The same with their leaders, too—let their leaders know what they should do to make this process work. In other words, with this learning initiative, what should [the executives] do? You need to make sure they encourage their practice leader to be at these meetings. They ought to ask their practice leader, when they come back from these things, "What are you going to do differently?" I think that is how you make this sustainable.

G: What is the value of this learning-based change initiative to this company?
P: First, you can go up and down the line with some of the value that it brings; it builds the competencies of the professional staff; it gets them talking the same language; it builds networks so it reduces efforts that are out there but increases effectiveness for these folks. I think another offshoot of this is that it is teaching them how you can balance the polarity of autonomy. They are learning that they can be autonomous yet there can be a centralized effort like

this that they can actually get value from to change things. So I think that may not be a direct, bottom-line value, but I think in the end it is a tangible one.

G: What mistakes have you made in the process? What would you do differently?

P: I think I would have initially had the meetings closer together. We are now doing it quarterly, and I think that it's okay, but in the beginning the meetings should have been more frequent. Although I don't know if I would have had the resources for that to happen. I probably would have also been more active in, and I hate to say holding the team leaders accountable, but following up with them to know how they are articulating this effort to their people and to their senior leaders. Another thing I would change is to have been a more active participant with them, shoulder to shoulder, in explaining the effort to their groups.

G: Did the facilitator [Greg] have any effect in this project in the beginning?

P: Yeah, I think obviously you have because they gave you a nickname. They recognize what you brought to the table. They understood your role, and they accepted that role. They listened to you about the process we have been going through. Anytime you get a diverse group like that and you walk away with a good nickname, I think that shows a positive impact.

G: What would you say are the characteristics or the things that allowed that acceptance to emerge?

P: One, you didn't pretend to know their business. You made it very clear what your expertise was and what their expertise was and what you were there to do. So they did not feel like, "Here is a guy who knows a little about my business, and now he is going to try to tell me the secrets to what I have been doing for the last twenty years. No way." That made a big difference—that you treated them as intelligent professionals in their area of expertise. You let them know that you had an area of expertise that they needed to be intelligent enough to take and learn to apply to make their business better. I think that was the big key.

G: Let's talk about you as the leader of this effort, because you have taken a much more facilitative approach to leading this particular change process. As a part of that preparation, you have tried to have a pretty holistic focus on yourself, on other people, on behaviors, thinking processes,

emotional processes—all those kinds of things. Has your awareness of your emotional process changed as you have led this effort? If so, how?

P: Yeah, it has. I think I am probably more open to at least understanding different points of view. I am more patient in letting people make their point. I am not as worried about finding the right answer as opposed to looking at all the right answers that are available. I understand that there may not be just one. That was a big change for me.

G: Has your thinking process or your assumptions changed? If so, how?

P: My thinking process has definitely changed. While sitting in meetings with groups of people, I find myself questioning why I am thinking what I am thinking. What is driving me to think that? Then getting to that point and defining that for myself. Then asking the other people, "Why are you thinking what you are thinking?" So yeah, it has definitely changed.

G: Has it affected the way you interact with others? If so, how?

P: Yeah, outside the group it is the same thing. I guess I am more reflective internally. I am not as quick to make my point as I am to sit back and challenge my point and bounce it against the other points being made.

G: What benefits have you experienced in doing that?

P: I don't get as disappointed as often because I try to understand and I can go with another person's point of view or a combination of their view and my view. I don't get as frustrated when they don't see what I am saying. Probably the biggest thing is asking the right questions. Senior leaders and other key leaders in other companies ask good questions. I don't know if they innately do this or if they have gone through some process like this, but I think asking better questions, and not necessarily the most correct and deepest, but just better questions.

G: Tell me if outside of this learning initiative, you are applying this process. We are talking about it here, and it seems that you are applying it other places. Are there any illustrations of how you have done that and the outcomes?

P: I think probably the biggest and clearest illustration has been that a big company planning process has fallen to me. That effort started out as an internal company effort with IT [Information Technology] professionals from every group within the company. Then, myself and Audit got in that group. We started talking about virtual teams and learning teams and how you can have the autonomy but have an enterprise effort. That process probably went on for eight or nine months. I think the reason it fell to me was that I was being recognized as more of a facilitator than a kingdom builder. It came down to the point, without me ever articulating any desire to have this role, that they said they thought I should have it. I think that is a direct outcome of starting this learning effort with the safety group.

G: Are you experiencing a lot of the same results?
P: Yeah. I think probably in a much more accelerated fashion. It is not a totally facilitative role. There is some direct control. But taking that control and putting it in the back seat and approaching it more from a learning aspect has probably accelerated some of the outcomes that we are starting to see with this group.

G: How is this learning process and the learning model affected your thinking on leadership?
P: Well, again, I think when you look at some of the truly great leaders, they are more facilitative and reflective. It doesn't mean they get their groups to sit around, hold hands and just sing songs. But I think that the role of a leader as facilitator is probably more powerful in the long run than the person who makes command decisions on their own.

Notes

Introduction

1. D. Hock, *Birth of the Chaordic Age* (San Francisco: Berrett-Koehler Publishers, 1999).

Chapter 1

1. E. Friedman, *A Failure of Nerve: Leadership in the Age of the Quick Fix* (Bethesda, Maryland: The Edwin Friedman Estate/Trust, 1999).
2. Ibid., 13.
3. Arbinger Institute, *Leadership and Self-Deception* (San Francisco: Berrett-Koehler, 2000).
4. R. E. Quinn, *Change the World* (San Francisco: Jossey-Bass, 2000).

Chapter 2

1. Scharmer, 1999.
2. E. Friedman, *A Failure of Nerve: Leadership in the Age of the Quick Fix.*
3. P. Steinke, *How Your Church Family Works: Understanding Congregations as Emotional Systems* (New York: The Alban Institute, 1993).
4. D. Tutu, *No Future Without Forgiveness* (New York: Doubleday, 1999).
5. Ibid.
6. Ibid.
7. M. Lapsley, "Confronting the Past and Creating the Future: The Redemptive Value of Truth Telling," *Social Research,* 65, 4 (1998): 741-759.
8. P. van Zyl, "Dilemmas of Transitional Justice: The Case of South Africa's Truth and Reconciliation Commission," *Journal of International Affairs,* 52, 2 (1999): 648-669.

9. Lapsley, "Confronting the Past and Creating the Future: The Redemptive Value of Truth Telling."
10. Hamber, 2000.

Chapter 3
1. T. Brooks, *The Scions of Shannara* (New York: Del Rey, 1990).
2. M. S. Peck, *The Different Drum: Community Making and Peace* (New York: Touchstone, 1987).
3. M. Wheatley and M. Kellner-Rogers, "Bringing life to organizational change," *Journal for Strategic Performance Measurement,* (1998): 5-14.
4. P. Jackson and H. Delehanty, *Sacred Hoops: Spiritual Lessons of a Hardwood Warrior* (New York: Hyperion, 1995), 4.
5. M. Jordan, *For the Love of the Game* (New York: Crown Publishers, Inc, 1998), 59.
6. W. Isaacs, *Dialogue and the Art of Thinking Together* (New York: Doubleday, 1999).
7. E. Friedman, *A Failure of Nerve: Leadership in the Age of the Quick Fix.*
8. Peck, *The Different Drum: Community Making and Peace.*
9. H. Nouwen, *Reaching Out* (New York: Image, 1975).
10. P. Jackson and H. Delehanty, *Sacred Hoops: Spiritual Lessons of a Hardwood Warrior,* 156.
11. Friedman, *A Failure of Nerve: Leadership in the Age of the Quick Fix.*
12. M. Wheatley and P. Chodron, "It Starts with Uncertainty: Margaret Wheatley & Pema Chodron on Leading by Letting Go," <www.berkana. org/articles/uncertainty.html>, 7 March 2000, 1-7.

Chapter 4
1. J. Campbell, *The Hero's Journey: Joseph Campbell on His Life and Work,* edited by Phil Cousineau (New York: HarperCollins, 1999).

Chapter 5
1. E. Friedman, *Reinventing Leadership* (New York: Guliford Publications, 1996).
2. D. Bohm, *On Dialogue* (London: Routledge, 1996).
3. M. E. Kerr and M. Bowen, *Family Evaluation* (New York: W. W. Norton, 1988).
4. W. Isaacs, *Dialogue and the Art of Thinking Together.*
5. H. Nouwen, *The Way of the Heart* (San Francisco: Harper, 1981).
6. L. Bolman and T. Deal, *Leading with Soul* (San Francisco: Jossey-Bass, 1995).

7. M. Kets de Vries, *Leaders, Fools and Impostors: Essays on the Psychology of Leadership* (San Francisco: Jossey-Bass, 1993).

8. P. Palmer, *Let Your Life Speak* (San Francisco: Jossey-Bass, 2000).

9. Ibid.

10. Ibid.

11. E. Friedman, *A Failure of Nerve: Leadership in the Age of the Quick Fix.*

12. R. Reiner (Producer and Director) *The American President* (1995) ASIN 6305132666.

13. Friedman, *Reinventing Leadership;* Friedman, *A Failure of Nerve: Leadership in the Age of the Quick Fix.*

14. Friedman, *A Failure of Nerve: Leadership in the Age of the Quick Fix.*

15. Friedman, *Reinventing Leadership.*

16. B. Boyle and M. Taylor (Producers) J. Turteltaub (Director) *Instinct* (1999) ASIN 6305608253.

17. Palmer, *Let Your Life Speak,* 60.

18. J. Jaworski, *Synchronicity: The Inner Path of Leadership* (San Francisco: Berrett-Koehler, 1996).

19. See, for example, G. Bateson, *Steps to an Ecology of Mind* (New York: E. P. Dutton, 1972); Bohm, *On Dialogue;* Kerr and Bowen, *Family Evaluation;* P. Senge, *The Fifth Discipline* (New York: Doubleday, 1990).

20. See, for example, A. de Gues, *The Living Company* (Boston: Harvard Business School Press, 1997); E. Friedman, *Generation to Generation* (New York: Guliford Press, 1985); Friedman, *A Failure of Nerve: Leadership in the Age of the Quick Fix;* D.K. Hurst, *Crisis and Renewal* (Boston: Harvard Business School Press, 1995); M. McMaster, *The Intelligence Advantage: Organizing for Complexity* (Boston: Butterworth-Heinemann, 1996); M. Wheatley, *Leadership and the New Science* (San Francisco: Berrett-Koehler, 1992); D. Zohar, *Rewiring the Corporate Brain* (San Francisco: Berrett-Koehler, 1997).

21. M. Wheatley and M. Kellner-Rogers, *A Simpler Way* (San Francisco: Berrett-Koehler, 1996).

Chapter 6

1. W. Isaacs, *Dialogue and the Art of Thinking Together.*

2. Ibid.

3. H. Nouwen, *Letters to Marc about Jesus* (San Francisco: Harper & Row, 1987).

4. G. Robinson, "Contemporary Spiritual Pathologies—Implications for Personal and Organizational Change," *Peer Day Report,* 1999.

5. Ibid.

6. B. Johnson, *Polarity Management* (Amherst, MA: HRD Press, 1992).

7. Ibid.
8. Ibid.
9. Ibid.
10. M. Jordan, *For the Love of the Game*, 53.
11. E. Friedman, *A Failure of Nerve: Leadership in the Age of the Quick Fix*.
12. Ibid.

Chapter 8
1. Internal Company Report, 1999.

Epilogue
1. See, for example, A. de Gues, *The Living Company* (Boston: Harvard Business School Press, 1997); D. Hock, *Birth of the Chaordic Age*; M. Wheatley, *Leadership and the New Science*; M. Wheatley, and M. Kellner-Rogers, *A Simpler Way*; D. Zohar, *Rewiring the Corporate Brain*.
2. G. Morgan, *Images of Organization* (Thousand Oaks, CA: Sage, 1998).
3. C. S. Chivvis, "The Ascent of the Nation-State," *World & I*, 14, 3 (1999): 18-30.
4. R. Tarnas, *The Passion of the Western Mind: Understanding the Ideas That Have Shaped Our Worldview* (New York: Ballantine Books, 1991); G. Tyler, "Evolution of a Millennium," *New Leader*, 82, 12 (1999): 11-15.
5. R. Capon, *The Astonished Heart* (Grand Rapids, MI: Eerdmans, 1996) 64.
6. Ibid.
7. Tarnas, *The Passion of the Western Mind: Understanding the Ideas That Have Shaped Our Worldview*.
8. Ibid.
9. Ibid.
10. Ibid.
11. Ibid.
12. Ibid.
13. J.W. Kremer, "The Dark Night of the Scholar: Reflections on Culture and Ways of Knowing," *ReVision*, 14, 4 (1992): 169-179; T. Umehara, "The Civilization of the Forest," *NPQ: New Perspectives Quarterly*, 16, 2 (1999): 40-49.
14. T. Berry, *The Great Work* (New York: Bell Tower, 1999).
15. R. Capon, *The Astonished Heart*.
16. C. S. Chivvis, "The Ascent of the Nation-State."
17. J. White, "National Communism and World Revolution: The Political Consequences of German Military Withdrawal from the Baltic Area in 1918–19," *Europe-Asia Studies*, 46, 8 (1994): 1349-1370.

18. R. Shareef, "Ecovision: A Leadership Theory for Innovative Organizations," *Organizational Dynamics*, 20, 1 (1991): 50-63.
19. D. Quinn, *Beyond Civilization* (New York: Harmony Books, 1999).
20. V. Mastny, "The Soviet Non-Invasion of Poland in 1980-1981 and the End of the Cold War," *Europe-Asia Studies*, 51, 2 (1999): 190-213.
21. M. Freeman, "Scientific Management: 100 Years Old; Poised for the Next Century," *S.A.M. Advanced Management Journal*, 61, 2 (1996): 35-42.
22. G. Tyler, "Evolution of a Millennium."
23. D. Quinn, *Ishmael* (New York: Bantam Books, 1992).
24. Ibid; D. Quinn, *Beyond Civilization*.
25. S. Abdullah, *Creating a World that Works for All* (San Francisco: Berrett-Koehler, 1999).
26. R. Shareef, "Ecovision: A Leadership Theory for Innovative Organizations."
27. Tarnas, *The Passion of the Western Mind: Understanding the Ideas That Have Shaped Our Worldview*.
28. Ibid.
29. Ibid.
30. Ibid.
31. Ibid.
32. E. Friedman, *Reinventing Leadership*.
33. M. Kets de Vries, *Leaders, Fools and Impostors: Essays on the Psychology of Leadership*.

Bibliography

Abdullah, Sharif M. *Creating a World that Works for All*. San Francisco: Berrett-Koehler, 1999.

Alber, A. M. "Differentiation of Self in Counselor Trainees and Correlates of Functional Position in the Family of Origin." Unpublished doctoral dissertation. University of South Carolina, Columbia, South Carolina, 1991.

American President, The [film]. 1995. Directed and produced by Rob Reiner. Distributed by Columbia Pictures.

Arbinger Institute. *Leadership and Self-Deception*. San Francisco: Berrett-Koehler, 2000.

Argyris, Chris. *Overcoming Organizational Defenses: Facilitating Organizational Learning*. Boston: Allyn and Bacon, 1990.

Barnett, Thomas P.M. *The Pentagon's New Map*. New York: G. P. Putnams Sons, 2004.

Bateson, Gregory. *Steps to an Ecology of Mind*. New York: E. P. Dutton, 1972.

Berry, Thomas. *The Great Work: Our Way into the Future*. New York: Bell Tower, 2000.

Bohm, David. *On Dialogue*. London: Routledge, 1996.

Bolman, Lee, and Terrence Deal. *Leading with Soul*. San Francisco: Jossey-Bass, 1995.

Bowen, Murray. *Family Therapy in Clinical Practice*. New York: Jason Aronson, 1978.

Brendler, B. "What's Wrong with Change Management." <www.crmguru.com/content/features/brendler02.html>, 1-6, 10 January 2001.

Brooks, Terry. *The Scions of Shannara.* New York: Del Rey, 1990.

Burke, R. "Culture's consequences: organizational values, satisfaction and performance." *Empowerment in Organizations,* (1995): 3-5.

Burton, A. "Operational theories of personality." In A. Ellis, *Rational-emotive Therapy.* New York: Brunner/Mazel, 1974.

Bynner, Witter. *The Way of Life, According to Lau Tzu.* New York: Perigee, 1986/1944.

Campbell, Joseph. *The Hero's Journey: Joseph Campbell on His Life and Work,* edited by Phil Cousineau. New York: HarperCollins, 1999.

Capon, Robert F. *The Parables of the Kingdom.* Grand Rapids, MI: Eerdmans, 1985.

Capon, Robert F. *The Parables of Grace.* Grand Rapids, MI: Eerdmans, 1988.

Capon, Robert F. *The Mystery of Christ and Why We Don't Get It.* Grand Rapids, MI: Eerdmans, 1993.

Capon, Robert F. *The Astonished Heart.* Grand Rapids, MI: Eerdmans, 1996.

Capon, Robert F. *The Foolishness of Preaching: Proclaiming the Gospel Against the Wisdom of the World.* Grand Rapids, MI: Eerdmans, 1998.

Carpenter, M. C. "A Test of Bowen Family Systems Theory: The Relationship of Differentiation of Self and Chronic Anxiety." Unpublished doctoral dissertation, University of Maryland, College Park, 1990.

Chivvis, C. S. "The Ascent of the Nation-State." *World & I,* 14, no. 3 (1999): 18-30.

Covey, Stephen R. *The Seven Habits of Highly Effective People.* New York: Fireside, 1989.

Cowan, D. A. "Rhythms of Learning: Patterns that Bridge Individuals and Organizations." *Journal of Management Inquiry,* 4 no. 3 (1995): 222-237.

Cranton, Patricia. *Understanding and Promoting Transformative Learning.* San Francisco: Jossey-Bass, 1994.

De Gues, Arie. *The Living Company.* Boston: Harvard Business School Press, 1997.

Ellinor, Linda, and Glenna Gerard. *Dialogue.* New York: John Wiley & Sons, 1998.

Freeman, M. "Scientific Management: 100 Years Old; Poised for the Next Century." *S.A.M. Advanced Management Journal,* 61, no. 2 (1996): 35-42.

Friedman, Edwin H. *Generation to Generation.* New York: Guliford Press, 1985.

Friedman, Edwin H. *Family Process and Process Theology: Basic New Concepts.* Washington DC: The Alban Institute, 1991.

Friedman, Edwin H. *Reinventing Leadership.* New York: Guliford Publications, 1996.

Friedman, Edwin H. *A Failure of Nerve: Leadership in the Age of the Quick Fix.* Bethesda, Maryland: The Edwin Friedman Estate/Trust, 1999.

George, Rickey L., and T. S. Cristiani. *Counseling Theory & Practice.* Englewood Cliffs, New Jersey: Prentice-Hall, Inc, 1986.

Gibson, Rowan. *Rethinking the Future.* London: Nicholas Brealey Publishing, 1997.

Heller, A. "The Three Logics of Modernity and the Double Bind." <http://hi.rutgers.edu/szelenyi60/heller.html>, 1-13, 8 March 2000.

Hock, Dee. "The one horned cow." <www.chaordic.org/chaordic/the_one_horned_cow.htm>, 1999.

Hock, Dee. *Birth of the Chaordic Age.* San Francisco: Berrett-Koehler Publishers, 1999.

House, R. J., and R. N. Aditya. "The social scientific study of leadership: quo vadis?" *Journal of Management,* 23, no. 3 (1997): 409-474.

Hunter, Paul. "Executive Report to Williams Executive Committee." 1999.

Hurst, David K. *Crisis and Renewal.* Boston: Harvard Business School Press, 1995.

Instinct [film]. Directed by Jon Turteltaub. Produced by Barbara Boyle and Michael Taylor. Distributed by Touchstone Pictures, 1999.

Isaacs, William. *Dialogue: The Art of Thinking Together.* New York: Doubleday. 1999.

Jackson, Phil, and Hugh Delehanty. *Sacred Hoops: Spiritual Lessons of a Hardwood Warrior.* New York: Hyperion, 1995.

Jaworski, Joseph. *Synchronicity: The Inner Path of Leadership.* San Francisco: Berrett-Koehler, 1996.

Johnson, Barry. *Polarity Management.* Amherst, MA: HRD Press, 1992.

Jordan, Michael. *For the Love of the Game.* New York: Crown Publishers, Inc, 1998.

Juechter, M., C. Fisher, and A. Alford, "Five Conditions for High-Performing Cultures," <www.astd.org/CMS/templates/template_1.html>, 1-8, 29 June 1998.

Kerr, Michael E., and Murray Bowen. *Family Evaluation.* New York: W. W. Norton, 1988.

Kets de Vries, Manfred F. R. *Leaders, Fools and Impostors: Essays on the Psychology of Leadership.* San Francisco: Jossey-Bass, 1993.

Koestenbaum, Peter. *Leadership: The Inner Side of Greatness.* San Francisco: Jossey-Bass, 1991.

Kremer, J. W. "The Dark Night of the Scholar: Reflections on Culture and Ways of Knowing." *ReVision,* 14, no. 4 (1992): 169-179.

Lapsley, M. "Confronting the Past and Creating the Future: The Redemptive Value of Truth Telling." *Social Research,* 65, no. 4 (1998): 741-759.

Mastny, V. "The Soviet Non-Invasion of Poland in 1980-1981 and the End of the Cold War." *Europe-Asia Studies,* 51, no. 2(1999): 190-213.

McMaster, Michael D. *The Intelligence Advantage: Organizing for Complexity.* Boston: Butterworth-Heinemann, 1996.

Metzner, Ralph. *The Unfolding Self.* Novato, CA: Origin Press, 1986

Mezirow, Jack. *Transformative Dimensions of Adult Learning.* San Francisco: Jossey-Bass, 1991.

Morgan, Gareth. *Images of Organization.* Thousand Oaks, CA: Sage, 1998.

Nouwen, Henri. *Creative Ministry.* New York: Doubleday, 1971.

Nouwen, Henri. *Reaching Out.* New York: Image, 1975.

Nouwen, Henri. *The Way of the Heart.* San Francisco: Harper, 1981.

Nouwen, Henri. *Letters to Marc about Jesus.* San Francisco: Harper & Row, 1987.

Nouwen, Henri. *In the Name of Jesus.* New York: Crossroad, 1989.

Olson, Edwin E., and Glenda. H. Eoyang. *Facilitating Organization Change.* San Francisco: Jossey-Bass, 2001.

Oshry, Barry. *Leading Systems.* San Francisco: Berrett-Koehler, 1999.

Palmer, Parker J. *The Courage to Teach.* San Francisco: Jossey-Bass, 1998.

Palmer, Parker J. *Let Your Life Speak.* San Francisco: Jossey-Bass, 2000.

Peck, M. Scott. *The Different Drum: Community Making and Peace.* New York: Touchstone, 1987.

Peterson, Eugene H. *Working the Angles.* Grand Rapids, MI: Eerdmans, 1987.

Peterson, Eugene H. *Under the Unpredictable Plant.* Grand Rapids, MI: Eerdmans, 1992.

Peterson, Eugene H. *Subversive Spirituality.* Vancouver: Regent College Bookstore, 1994.

Quinn, Daniel. *Ishmael.* New York: Bantam Books, 1992.

Quinn, Daniel. *Beyond Civilization.* New York: Harmony Books, 1999.

Quinn, Robert E. *Deep Change.* San Francisco: Jossey-Bass, 1996.

Quinn, Robert E. *Change the World.* San Francisco: Jossey-Bass, 2000.

Richardson, Ronald W. *Creating a Healthier Church.* Minneapolis: Fortress Press, 1996.

Robinson, Greg. "Peer Day Report: Contemporary Spiritual Pathologies— Implications for Personal and Organizational Change," 1999.

Robinson, Greg. *Teams for a New Generation: An Introduction to Collective Learning.* Tulsa, OK: BDI, 2000.

Roos, J., and M. Lissack. "Getting Your Act Together: Mastering Corporate Complexity through Coherence." <http://coherence.org/PFM.htm>, 1-5, 14 May 2000.

Roth, George, and Art Kleiner. *Car Launch: The Human Side of Managing Change*. New York: Oxford University Press, 2000.

Rough, J. "Dynamic facilitation and the magic of self-organizing change," <www.tobe.net/papers/facilitn.htm>, 15 July 1999.

Schein, E. H. "Culture: the missing concept in organization studies." *Administrative Science Quarterly*, 41, no. 2 (1996): 229- 241.

Senge, Peter. *The Fifth Discipline*. New York: Doubleday, 1990.

Shareef, R. "Ecovision: A Leadership Theory for Innovative Organizations." *Organizational Dynamics*, 20, no. 1 (1991): 50-63.

Steinke, Peter L. *How Your Church Family Works: Understanding Congregations as Emotional Systems*. New York: The Alban Institute, 1993.

Steinke, Peter L. *Healthy Congregations: A Systems Approach*. New York: Alban Institute, 1996.

Strauss, William, and Neil Howe. *The Fourth Turning*. New York: Broadway Books, 1997.

Strong, James. *Strong's Exhaustive Concordance of the Bible*. Nashville: Thomas Nelson, 1984.

Tarnas, Richard. *The Passion of the Western Mind: Understanding the Ideas That Have Shaped Our Worldview*. New York: Ballantine Books, 1991.

Taylor, E. W. "Building upon the Theoretical Debate: A Critical Review of the Empirical Studies of Mezirow's Transformative Learning Theory." *Adult Education Quarterly*, 48 (1998): 34-60.

Tichy, Noel M., and Eli Cohen. *The Leadership Engine*. New York: Harper Business, 1997.

Toynbee, Arnold J. *Change and Habit: The Challenge of Our Time*. New York: Oxford University Press, 1966.

Tutu, Desmond. *No Future Without Forgiveness*. New York: Doubleday, 1999.

Tyler, G. "Evolution of a Millennium." *New Leader*, 82, no. 12 (1999): 11-15.

Umehara, T. "The Civilization of the Forest." *NPQ: New Perspectives Quarterly*, 16, no. 2 (1999): 40-49.

van Zyl, P. "Dilemmas of Transitional Justice: The Case of South Africa's Truth and Reconciliation Commission." *Journal of International Affairs*, 52, no. 2 (1999): 648-669.

Wheatley, Margaret. *Leadership and the New Science*. San Francisco: Berrett-Koehler, 1992.

Wheatley, Margaret, and Myron Kellner-Rogers. "Bringing life to organizational change." *Journal for Strategic Performance Measurement,* (1998): 5-14.

Wheatley, Margaret, and Myron Kellner-Rogers. *A Simpler Way.* San Francisco: Berrett-Koehler, 1996.

Wheatley, Margaret, and Pema Chodron. "It Starts with Uncertainty: Margaret Wheatley & Pema Chodron on Leading by Letting Go." <www.berkana. org/articles/uncertainty.html>, 1-7, 7 March 2000.

White, J. "National Communism and World Revolution: The Political Consequences of German Military Withdrawal from the Baltic Area in 1918–19." *Europe-Asia Studies,* 46, no. 8 (1994): 1349-1370.

Zohar, Danah. *Rewiring the Corporate Brain.* San Francisco: Berrett-Koehler, 1997.

About the Authors

Greg Robinson is currently President of Challenge Quest, LLC in Pryor, Oklahoma. Previous to coming to Challenge Quest, Greg spent 5 years with Williams in Tulsa, Oklahoma as a Managing Organization Development Consultant.

Greg has a Ph.D. in Organizational Behavior and Leadership from The Union Institute and University in Cincinnati, Ohio. He also has a M.S. in Counseling from John Brown University.

Greg's professional career has concentrated in the areas of team development, leadership development, facilitation and consulting with organizational change efforts. His first book was *Teams for a New Generation: An Introduction to Collective Learning*. This book is a "how to" to develop the four distinct abilities needed to build the infrastructure for teams to learn collectively.

Greg currently resides with his wife Jeannie, his daughter Keely and son Kobe in Pryor, Oklahoma.
greg@challengequest.com

About the Authors

Mark Rose is the Business Development Leader for Challenge Quest, LLC. His main focus is equipping teams with skills and tools to become more effective. He received his Master's of Human Relations degree from The University of Oklahoma.

Mark is a national ASTD member and 2004 VP of Programming for the Central Oklahoma ASTD Chapter. He has worked as co-facilitator in a series of training videos, *Trainer Games in Action: Volume One and Two* which show how trainers can use activities to help the retention of information for their learners. Both videos received ASTD's Central Oklahoma Chapter Award of Excellence.

Mark is a certified challenge course instructor who has worked in the experiential learning field with clients in non-profit companies, government agencies and corporations. He is a skilled facilitator, and excels in his ability to enable clients to relate challenge course behaviors to actual work and home behaviors.

He completed his Certificate of Achievement from the University of Oklahoma's Training and Development Certificate Program and currently teaches in the program. He enjoys golfing and spending time outdoors with his wife and two daughters.
mark@challengequest.com

Printed in the United States
43095LVS00005B/130-228